THE CHRISTMAS FAMILY TREE

The Christmas Family Tree
Advent Through the Ancestry of Christ

978-1-7910-4390-2

978-1-7910-4391-9 eBook

Also from Benjamin Crismon

40 Days: A Lenten Journey Through Exodus

Cover description: Features a stylized Christmas tree formed from illustrated figures in Jesus's genealogy, arranged on horizontal branches beneath a gold star. The tree begins with Abraham and Isaac at the top and continues through biblical ancestors including Jacob, Judah, Rahab, Ruth, David, Solomon, Josiah, Zerubbabel, and Joseph, ending above a simple manger. The title, *The Christmas Family Tree*, appears in large red sans serif uppercase letters, with the subtitle, *Advent Through the Ancestry of Christ*, in green serif type to the right of the tree. The author's name, Benjamin Crismon, appears in green serif letters at the bottom.

THE CHRISTMAS FAMILY TREE

Advent Through the Ancestry of Christ

BENJAMIN CRISMON

Abingdon Press | Nashville

The Christmas Family Tree
Advent Through the Ancestry of Christ

Library of Congress Control Number: 2026943075
978-1-7910-4390-2

MANUFACTURED IN THE UNITED STATES OF AMERICA

CONTENTS

Introduction 7
Day 1 10
Day 2 14
Day 3 20
Day 4 25
Day 5 30
Day 6 35
Day 7 40
Day 8 45
Day 9 51
Day 10 57
Day 11 62
Day 12 68
Day 13 73
Day 14 78
Day 15 83
Day 16 89
Day 17 96
Day 18 101
Day 19 106
Day 20 112
Day 21 118
Day 22 123
Day 23 128
Day 24 135
Day 25 142

INTRODUCTION

The Christmas season often finds us with family and friends, gathered around Christmas trees decked out in lights, surrounded by beautiful decorations, and overflowing with ornaments that tell the stories of our heritage and tradition. These gatherings are different from our typical ones—more people, more gifts, more laughter, more joy. There's something sacred about the shared space around the Christmas tree. It becomes a place where memories are made, stories are passed down, and love is both spoken and shared.

One of my favorite Christmas movies, *National Lampoon's Christmas Vacation*, tells the story of the extended Griswold family, all crammed under one roof for the holidays. Grandparents, aunts and uncles, crazy cousins, and angsty in-laws—each one with their own quirks—come together to try and capture the beauty and chaos of the season. It's hilarious, heartwarming, and sometimes a little too relatable. The movie works because it tells the truth: Families are never perfect, but they can be full of meaning and love. Christmas, at its best, brings us back together—not just in proximity but in heart.

There's a particular kind of magic that happens when we reunite with the people we love, even if it's just once a year. It's in those moments that we hear old stories told again, stories that somehow feel brand new when wrapped in memory and laughter. We hear about grandparents who shaped us, great-aunts whose recipes still show up at every holiday meal, and siblings who once shared bunk beds and now share parenting advice. These are the people who made us who we are. These are the voices that echo through the generations.

In the same way, the story of Jesus doesn't happen in a vacuum. His arrival in Bethlehem isn't disconnected from what came before; it's the culmination of a long and winding family story. This Advent, we are going to pull up a few more chairs to our tree and invite some new old faces to join us. We'll spend time with the ancestors of Jesus, those faithful and flawed men and women who show up in the genealogies recorded in the Gospels of Matthew and Luke. These aren't just names on a list—they're real people with real stories, people God used to prepare the way for the birth of Christ. We will also look to the stories of those connected to the birth of Jesus and hear how their lives of faith speak deeply into our own.

Some of them became heroes of the faith. Others made terrible mistakes. Some did both. Some were outsiders grafted in by grace. Some led boldly; others quietly influenced the course of history. But together, they form the spiritual family that God worked through to bring hope into the world. Their stories are filled with promise and pain, redemption and risk, courage and compromise. In their stories, we find echoes of our own.

So this Advent season, I invite you to think about the ancestors of Jesus and how their stories point us to the true meaning of Christmas. Through the Scriptures, Abraham and Rebekah, Jacob and Judah, Ruth and Rahab, Boaz and David, and even a lesser-known figure like Zerubbabel become gifts to us, showing us how God has been at work in the world for generations, giving intimations, indications, and prophecies of Christ's entrance into the world—Godself becoming part of our human family.

This book is intended to be read as a personal devotional or as a group resource. In each chapter, we will walk through the stories of different characters and you will find questions that guide further introspection or discussion.

The halls are decked, the cider is warm on the stovetop, and the ham is almost ready. Our guests are beginning to arrive. Let's welcome them into our hearts, our homes, and our lives. And as we do, may we prepare not only to celebrate the birth of Christ but also to make room for his story in our story—again and again.

DAY 1

ABRAHAM

Now the LORD said to Abram, "Go from your country and your kindred and your father's house to the land that I will show you. I will make of you a great nation, and I will bless you and make your name great, so that you will be a blessing. I will bless those who bless you, and the one who curses you I will curse, and in you all the families of the earth shall be blessed."

So Abram went, as the LORD had told him, and Lot went with him. Abram was seventy-five years old when he departed from Haran. Abram took his wife Sarai and his brother's son Lot and all the possessions that they had gathered and the persons whom they had acquired in Haran, and they set forth to go to the land of Canaan.

Genesis 12:1-5

Abraham is often called the father of our faith, and for good reason. In Matthew's telling of Jesus's genealogy, his is the very first name mentioned. Not Adam, not Noah—Abraham. That's a statement. It tells us that Abraham's story marks a defining moment in our family's spiritual history. He is the patriarch of the promise, the man who walked away from everything familiar because he trusted in a God who promised something better.

Abraham didn't start with a clear plan. He didn't have a map or a five-year plan. What he had was a voice—a divine calling—and enough faith to follow it. He left his homeland, his kindred, and his security to pursue a future he couldn't yet see. That kind of faith is what sets the table for the rest of the story. He becomes not only the biological ancestor of the people of Israel but also the spiritual ancestor of all who live by faith. He is the one through whom God promises to bless all the families of the earth. That includes yours and mine.

In so many ways, Abraham reminds me of the patriarchs in our own families. For me, it's my grandfather Pedro—"Pebo" to those of us who adored him. He died when I was six, but the impression he left was deep and lasting. I remember Christmases at Pebo's house in Pocahontas, Arkansas—days filled with card games, food, laughter, and warmth. I can still picture myself sitting on his lap at the kitchen table as he dominated game after game of spades, delighting in every win.

One of the first gifts I really remember getting was my first bike, from none other than Pebo. I learned to ride in front of his house, on that long, flat driveway. I will never forget how safe and comforted I felt after my first fall as he scooped me up in his big, strong arms. That house, with its endless rooms and buzzing energy, felt like a palace to me. It's been decades since we gathered there, but those memories are a living part of who I am. I suspect you have someone like that too—someone whose faith or presence shaped your sense of what family means.

Abraham is that person for us spiritually. His faith set the course for generations. His obedience became the foundation of a nation. He didn't always get everything right—he made mistakes, took wrong turns, and sometimes tried to fulfill God's promise on his own terms. But still, God walked with him. God continued to bless him. And through that relationship, the covenant was formed: "I will bless you and . . . you will be a blessing" (Genesis 12:2). That's the heart of Abraham's legacy, and it is still the calling of every one of us who claims a seat at this table.

In Advent, we talk a lot about waiting and preparation, but we don't usually talk about courage even though courage is integral to the Christmas story, particularly on the part of Mary and Joseph. Likewise, Abraham had the courage to start something new, to build a legacy not just through bloodlines, but through belief. In the same way, this season calls us to courageous faith. We are invited not just to remember Christ's coming, but to live as if his return matters. That means living on mission, going where he sends us, and offering blessings in his name.

Maybe you're in a season where God is calling you into something new—a ministry, a risk, a relationship, a deeper step of obedience. Let Abraham's story remind you that faithful beginnings often look like uncertain steps. But those steps, taken in trust, become the very ground on which God builds something beautiful.

As we begin to discuss the ancestry of Jesus, it only makes sense to start with Abraham—the one who said yes before he had the full picture. So, let's listen closely to his story, seeing what lessons he has for us to learn. And let us not forget: We are still called, still blessed, and still sent into the world as a blessing to others.

- Does your family have an important patriarch or matriarch? What do you remember about them and their legacy?
- How have you been blessed by God to be a blessing to others?
- How can you be obedient to God's calling, like Abraham was, this Advent and Christmas season?

DAY 2

REBEKAH

When Abraham's servant heard their words, he bowed himself to the ground before the LORD. And the servant brought out jewelry of silver and of gold and garments and gave them to Rebekah; he also gave to her brother and to her mother costly ornaments. Then he and the men who were with him ate and drank, and they spent the night there. When they rose in the morning, he said, "Send me back to my master." Her brother and her mother said, "Let the young woman remain with us a while, at least ten days; after that she may go." But he said to them, "Do not delay me, since the LORD has made my journey successful; let me go that I may go to my master." They said, "We will call the young woman and ask her." And they called Rebekah and said to her, "Will you go with this man?" She said, "I will." So they sent away their sister Rebekah and her nurse along with Abraham's servant and his men.

Genesis 24:52-59

Rebekah, our first female ancestor, is next. She may not be the most famous name in the genealogy of Jesus, but she might be one of the boldest. She is far and away my favorite of the matriarchs.

Rebekah's moment of decision comes at a turning point in her life. A servant of Abraham's has arrived from a distant land with a strange and hopeful proposal: Would she be willing to leave everything—her family, her land, her language, and her customs? Would she be willing to travel to marry Isaac, a man she's never met?

Her father and brother call her in, "Will you go with this man?" And she answers with two small words that change the course of history: "I will."

Just like that. No hesitation. No bargaining. No long list of questions. "I will."

It's such a simple answer. But what it represents is anything but simple. It's an answer full of risk. Full of unknowns. Full of the kind of raw faith that Advent calls us to. It is the kind of faith that Mary had to have when the angel visited her. It is the kind of faith that we have to have to believe that the God of all creation stepped into humanity, into the mess of our story.

Rebekah's story is one of divine appointment, but it is also one of courageous consent. God may have set the wheels in motion, but her willingness becomes the hinge on which the promise swings forward. She is not coerced. She chooses; she goes.

There's a kind of courage embedded in her that often gets overlooked. In the biblical world, women rarely had agency over their future. And yet, here we have Rebekah, who offered her own decision, and she meets it with resolve. She steps out in faith not because she knows what's ahead, but because she trusts the One behind the calling.

I think of the women in my own life who've lived with that kind of resolve. My maternal grandmother, Roberta, comes to mind. She was a woman of deep wisdom and grit, the kind who knew how to fry up just about anything into a delicious meal. She could quilt, sew, and embroider. She also was a crack shot with a .22 rifle and would often have marksmanship competitions with her husband. I grew up hearing stories about her toughness, her loyalty, and her fierce love for her family. She wasn't the kind of person who sought recognition, but she was the kind of person people leaned on—because when she said "I will," she meant it. She said yes to hard seasons, yes to the messy, holy work of staying faithful when life didn't make it easy.

Rebekah feels like someone who would've gotten along with Roberta.

And maybe you've known a Rebekah too, someone whose quiet strength shaped your family. Someone who said yes to things that weren't guaranteed to turn out well, but they still said yes because they believed in love, in loyalty, in something bigger than themselves. Maybe that person is you. Maybe you're the one holding everything together right now with nothing more than faith and stubborn grace.

Rebekah's story reminds us that every spiritual journey requires a moment of surrender—a time when we choose to go not because we're certain but because we trust. Advent is full of those moments. God often calls us into unknown places, not always geographic places but more often emotional, relational, vocational ones. And we're faced with the same kind of question Rebekah heard: *Will you go? Will you forgive that person? Will you serve that neighbor? Will you pursue that call? Will you follow me?*

And here's the beauty: Rebekah didn't know how the story would unfold. She couldn't see that her willingness would help carry the promise forward, that her marriage would lead to Jacob, and Jacob to Judah, and Judah to David, and David to Jesus. She just knew it was time to go.

Sometimes we don't get the whole story. We just get a question. And like Rebekah, we're called to answer.

As I imagine her finding her place near the warmly lit tree at Christmas dinner, maybe beside Abraham or Ruth, I can picture her smile—warm, a little weathered, and full of quiet assurance. I imagine her hands resting on the table—hands that worked, hands that carried water from the well, hands that guided children, hands that held both grief and hope. Rebekah's life wasn't perfect. There's conflict later—favoritism, family tension, deception. She was human, like all of us. But none of that undoes the beauty of her first yes.

And isn't that the grace of Advent too? That our beginning yes can hold even when the journey gets messy?

This season, as we prepare to celebrate the arrival of Christ, Rebekah reminds us that preparation doesn't always mean having everything in order. Sometimes it means being willing to walk into the unknown. To let go of the comfortable. To choose trust over control.

We don't often think of Rebekah as a Christmas character. But maybe we should. Because the Christ Child comes into the world through a long line of people who said yes, people who trusted before they could see. Mary said yes. Joseph said yes. The shepherds said yes. And long before any of them, Rebekah whispered the words that echo through generations: "I will."

May her story nudge us to listen for the voice of God calling us forward. And when that moment comes, may we have the courage to respond not with all the answers but with all our hearts: "I will."

- What keeps you from saying yes to God when you hear God calling in your life?
- How can you tap into the faith of Rebekah that gave her the courage to leave her family and join a new one?
- What can you do this season to serve God better or in a new way?

DAY 3

JACOB

Jacob was left alone, and a man wrestled with him until daybreak. When the man saw that he did not prevail against Jacob, he struck him on the hip socket, and Jacob's hip was put out of joint as he wrestled with him. Then he said, "Let me go, for the day is breaking." But Jacob said, "I will not let you go, unless you bless me." So he said to him, "What is your name?" And he said, "Jacob." Then the man said, "You shall no longer be called Jacob, but Israel, for you have striven with God and with humans and have prevailed." Then Jacob asked him, "Please tell me your name." But he said, "Why is it that you ask my name?" And there he blessed him. So Jacob called the place Peniel, saying, "For I have seen God face to face, yet my life is preserved." The sun rose upon him as he passed Penuel, limping because of his hip.

Genesis 32:24-31

Jacob, one of Rebekah's sons, is the trickster, the heel-grabber, the younger brother who always wanted what wasn't his. He deceived his father, stole from his brother, ran away from consequences, and made messy choices that affected his whole family. And yet, Jacob is chosen. He's not just part of

Jesus's family line; he gives it a name: Israel. That name, the name of an entire nation, is born out of a night of wrestling, both literal and spiritual.

There's something about Jacob that many of us can relate to more than we'd like to admit. He's not heroic like Abraham or steady like Boaz. He's not remembered for a single bold act like Rahab or Rebekah. Instead, he's remembered for his struggle. For that long, painful, honest night where he finally stops running and wrestles with God. Not to win. Not to defeat. But to be blessed, to be changed.

I think about the people in our families who have had to fight for their faith. Not because they didn't believe, but because life made it hard to keep believing. Maybe they endured loss or disappointment or betrayal. Maybe they wandered and came back. Maybe they weren't the ones in church every Sunday, but when they did show up, you knew they were carrying something deeper than they let on.

In my own life, I've had those seasons too, the ones where I've prayed more out of desperation than devotion. Times when I felt like I was clinging to God not with perfect theology or joyful praise but with a stubborn hope that refused to let go. I've had moments when I wasn't sure what was ahead, but I knew I didn't want to face it without a blessing. Jacob reminds me that God honors that kind of fight.

There's this incredible moment in Jacob's story when God asks him, "What is your name?" (32:27). That might seem like a strange question. Of course God knows his name. But in the ancient world, your name was your identity. It wasn't just what people called you—it was who you were. And for Jacob to answer honestly was an act of confession. "Jacob" meant "deceiver," "grasper," "trickster." By naming himself, he's finally owning his past. And it's only after that bit of honesty that God gives him a new name: Israel. "You have striven with God and with humans and have prevailed" (32:28).

That's what grace looks like. Not a clean record, but a transformed identity.

I wonder what stories he would tell. I don't think he'd lead with the polished ones. I think he'd talk about the long walk back to reconcile with Esau. I think he'd tell us about falling in love with Rachel and getting tricked himself. I think he'd tell us what it feels like to live with the weight of your mistakes and the wonder of God loving you anyway.

And what a message that is for Advent. In a season when everything is polished and picturesque, when we decorate our homes and try to make our lives look photo-ready, Jacob's story reminds us that God doesn't wait for perfection. God meets us in the mess, in the wrestling, in the dark nights when we're alone with our questions. God doesn't just tolerate the wrestlers; he blesses them.

Maybe you're in a season like that now. Maybe you're holding on to God with more questions than answers. Maybe you've made some choices you regret, and you wonder if you still belong at the table. Jacob's life shouts, *Yes!* There is a place for you here. You don't have to be perfect to be used. You don't have to be unbroken to be blessed. You just have to keep holding on.

As we journey through Advent, we're reminded that Christ came into a world just like Jacob's—messy, struggling, full of broken people. And he came not just to forgive us but to give us a new name, a new identity, a new hope. That's what this season is about. Not just preparing to celebrate the baby in the manger but allowing ourselves to be transformed by the One who still meets us in the night.

Let's hear it for Jacob. He may not have it all together, but he's got something important to teach us. Let his limp remind us that wounds don't disqualify us from the blessing; they often lead us straight to it.

- Why do you think God never gave up on Jacob? What does that tell us about God?

- Have you ever felt like Jacob, scared that your past decisions have damaged your relationship with God?
- How can you accept God's forgiveness today and work to move forward into a renewed life of faith?

DAY 4

RAHAB

Before they went to sleep, [Rahab] came up to them on the roof and said to the men, "I know that the LORD has given you the land and that dread of you has fallen on us and that all the inhabitants of the land melt in fear before you. For we have heard how the LORD dried up the water of the Red Sea before you when you came out of Egypt and what you did to the two kings of the Amorites who were beyond the Jordan, to Sihon and Og, whom you utterly destroyed. As soon as we heard it, our hearts melted, and there was no courage left in any of us because of you. The LORD your God is indeed God in heaven above and on earth below. Now then, since I have dealt kindly with you, swear to me by the LORD that you in turn will deal kindly with my family."

Joshua 2:8-12

Rahab's name often comes with an asterisk. In Scripture, she's often called "Rahab the prostitute," as if that one word defines the whole of her. But that's not nearly the whole of her story. In fact, it's only the beginning. Rahab's presence in the genealogy of Jesus is one of the most powerful statements in all of Matthew's Gospel. She is a Gentile, a woman, and a former sex worker, and she is part of the Messiah's family line. Not as a footnote, not as a cautionary tale, but as a matriarch. But she's not a person we might expect to be there; only through her confidence and faith does she earn her place on this list.

Her story begins in Jericho, a city doomed to fall, with rumors of a God who rescues slaves and topples kings. When Israelite spies sneak into the city to scout it out, it's Rahab who hides them. It's Rahab who lies to protect them. It's Rahab who declares that their God—the God of Abraham, Isaac, and Jacob—is the true God of heaven and earth. That declaration is as bold as anything uttered by Israel's greatest prophets.

She says it not from the safety of a synagogue, but from the rooftop of her home, under threat of death, in a city preparing for war.

And she says it not because she's seen miracles with her own eyes, but because she's heard stories of them. That's what makes her faith so remarkable. She believes based on what she's heard. She aligns herself with the God of Israel long before she sees any proof that doing so will save her. While others cower in fear, Rahab chooses faith.

I think of the people in my life who've had to make decisions like that, bold choices based not on guarantees but on hope. People who left behind old lives to pursue something better, even when they had no reason to expect it would work out: immigrants, recovering addicts, single moms, new believers—people who saw the faint outline of grace on the horizon and stepped toward it, not knowing where the path would lead.

Rahab is one of them. She wasn't raised in the faith. She didn't grow up reciting the psalms or listening to the Torah. But something in her heart recognized truth when it knocked at her door. And so she opened it.

Scripture tells us that Rahab tied a scarlet cord in her window, a signal to the invading Israelites not to harm her household. That cord became the symbol of her faith, her protection, and her place in the story. It reminds us of another act involving a red sign, when the Israelites marked their doorposts with blood during the first Passover. The connection is thick with meaning. Her home is passed over. Her family is spared. A new future begins.

The thing I love most about Rahab is how quickly her past becomes irrelevant in the story of redemption. Yes, it's acknowledged. We're not asked to pretend it didn't happen. But the focus moves swiftly to her future. She becomes a part of Israel. She marries a man named Salmon. She gives birth to Boaz. That's right, *Boaz*, the man who will later marry Ruth, the man known for his kindness and honor. Don't tell me

Rahab didn't shape the next generation. The kindness Boaz shows to Ruth, the way he protects her dignity, the way he sees her worth—that kind of character is learned. And Boaz learned it from a mother who knew what it was like to be an outsider, a woman on the margins, and a soul redeemed by the mercy of God.

Rahab's presence at the Advent table is essential. She reminds us that faith doesn't begin with perfect theology; it begins with trust. That grace doesn't wait for cleaned-up lives; it moves right into the mess and starts building something holy. That God doesn't just forgive our past; he rewrites it into a future we never could have imagined.

Her story speaks volumes into this season. Advent is not for the pristine. It's for the searching. It's for those who are hanging on by a thread, listening for rumors of a God who saves, watching for signs of mercy in unexpected places. Rahab reminds us that Jesus didn't come to preserve a spotless bloodline. He came to redeem a broken one.

And if there's room in the line of Jesus for Rahab, then there is certainly room at Christ's table for us.

Because the truth is, Rahab is all of us. We're all holding onto cords of faith, trusting that the God we've heard about is the God who saves. We all come with our histories, our baggage, our quiet hopes that we might still be included. And Rahab's story whispers back: *You are.*

So let's welcome her message into our hearts. Let's honor her faith, her bravery, her willingness to believe in the God of heaven and earth. And let's remember, this story isn't just about where you've been. It's about where grace is leading you.

- Do you have any adopted or chosen family? What gifts does God share with you through them?
- Have you ever been the one invited into another family? How did that make you feel?
- In this Christmas season, how can you make more room at your table for those who might be missing that family connection this year?

DAY 5

JUDAH

Judah, your brothers shall praise you;
your hand shall be on the neck of your enemies;
your father's sons shall bow down before you.
Judah is a lion's whelp;
from the prey, my son, you have gone up.
He crouches down, he stretches out like a lion,
like a lioness—who dares rouse him up?
The scepter shall not depart from Judah,
nor the ruler's staff from between his feet,
until tribute comes to him,
and the obedience of the peoples is his.

Genesis 49:8-10

We don't get to know much about Judah, but what we can glean from a few stories displays a life of faith. Judah was the fourth son of Jacob and Leah, right in the middle of all of Jacob's sons. In a world dominated by the firstborn sons, Judah could have easily been lost to history, yet God had great things in store for him. Judah's name means "thanksgiving" or "praise," a name given by his mother that reflected her feelings toward God for the gift of her son. Judah embodied his name throughout his life. When Joseph's brothers clamored for his death, it was Judah who talked them into saving his life and selling him into slavery instead. His pragmatic leadership won him respect from his brother and foreshadowed his future. The tribe of Judah's descendants becomes one of the most prominent in Israelite history, living in his legacy.

Judah reminds me of a cousin of mine. He was effortlessly cool, engaging and smart, kind and funny. I always admired and looked up to him, as he is about ten years older than I am. His dad and my dad are first cousins and share a bond more like brothers. When he was in law school, often he would come over to our house for one of my mom's home-cooked meals and a chance to relax with family. I will never forget a few years later, when he allowed me the chance to drive his brand-new truck. I had never felt cooler than I did in that moment, driving my cousin around in his big, bad truck. But as time marched on, our families got together less and less, and my opportunities to be amazed by this cousin became more infrequent. Like Judah, I don't know him as well as other members of the family, but I still admire and appreciate his character and love of God and family. I know that he is a loving husband and devoted father, worthy of admiration. But at bottom, what made my cousin so special to me was his authenticity.

But Judah wasn't perfect. He had a deep moment of brokenness in dealing with his daughter-in-law Tamar, who was married to his son Er. After Er's death, following their traditions, Tamar married the second son, Onan. When Onan died, Judah refused to allow Selah, his third son, to marry Tamar. He should have taken her in and redeemed her with security and a future. Tamar, realizing the need to take drastic action, disguised herself, tricked Judah, and bore him twin sons, Perez and Zerah. Although he initially called for Tamar to be punished with death, Judah relents and confesses his misdeeds when he finds out he is the father. Judah realized the error of his ways and publicly confessed his wrongdoings. This account highlights themes of justice and redemption, as Perez becomes an ancestor of King David and, ultimately, Jesus Christ.

In our Scripture passage, we are reading his father's blessing over him, one of a great future filled with promise and divine purpose. This is not simply a hopeful wish but a prophetic word spoken over Judah's life, pointing toward leadership, strength, and influence among his brothers. That promise would take shape over generations as Judah rose to become one of the most abundant and powerful tribes in all of Israel. From this tribe would come King David, Israel's greatest king, further solidifying the importance of Judah's legacy in God's unfolding plan. Because of this, we will often hear the name of Judah throughout the Advent season, as so many prophecies about the coming Messiah are rooted in the promise that God's Anointed One would come from the tribe of Judah, a reminder that God's promises, once spoken, continue to bear fruit across generations.

Judah's story is a calling to us. It is a call to authenticity, being true to who God made us to be. Judah was created to be a leader, and despite his birth order, Judah faithfully rose to the occasion time and time again. That leadership was modeled fully in Judah's willingness to acknowledge his sinfulness, confess, and turn back to faith once again. As we continue to experience the coming of Jesus in our hearts, let us be a people who honor Judah's name by praising God in the bountiful times and the hard, giving thanks for what we have, what we have had, and what we trust God will give in the future. Let us be emboldened to take a stand for what is right and good, leading others into the light of Christ's love.

- Do you have a family member you wish you knew better? How could you connect with them?

- Do you feel like you are able to authentically be whom God created you to be? What keeps you from doing so?
- How do you praise God in the middle of the storms of life?

DAY 6

RUTH

Ruth said,

"Do not press me to leave you,
to turn back from following you!
Where you go, I will go;
where you lodge, I will lodge;
your people shall be my people
and your God my God.
Where you die, I will die,
and there will I be buried.
May the LORD do thus to me,
and more as well,
if even death parts me from you!"

Ruth 1:16-17

Ruth's story begins in grief. She's a foreigner, a Moabite, and a widow. She's lost her husband. She has no children. She stands in that haunting space where her past is gone, and her future has no clear shape. But instead of turning inward or returning to the comfort of her homeland, Ruth makes a decision that rewrites her future, and ours.

"Where you go, I will go" (1:16).

With those words, Ruth binds herself to Naomi, her mother-in-law, and to the people of Israel. But even more than that, she binds herself to the God of Israel. It's a radical act of love and conversion, all in one breath. She steps out of everything familiar and walks into a land, a culture, and a religion that are not her own, because loyalty means more to her than security.

There's something about Ruth's voice in this moment that stirs the soul. It's poetic, yes. But it's also gutsy. She isn't just committing to Naomi's household; she's pledging her whole life to God's unfolding story. She does this not with theological treatises or doctrinal creeds, but with a promise lived out in grit and grace.

I think of the people in my life who love like that, people who stay when it would be easier to leave. People who show up and keep showing up, who bind themselves to their families or their churches or their callings not because it's easy but because it's right.

Years ago, I met a woman in our church who reminded me so much of Ruth. She wasn't loud or pushy. But she was always there. She brought meals to new moms, sat with grieving widows, and taught Sunday school even when no one signed up to help. No big speeches. Just presence. Over and over again.

When her own husband passed away, she kept showing up, arms open, eyes clear, heart full. She modeled the idea that love is what you do on the days you'd rather not. Ruth would've believed in that.

What's extraordinary about Ruth is how ordinary her love looks. She doesn't slay a giant. She doesn't part a sea. She doesn't call fire from heaven. She walks beside an old woman on a dusty road to Bethlehem. She gleans in fields. She works hard. She risks her reputation and follows Naomi's plan to approach Boaz. Her faithfulness is lived out in long days and hard choices. And that's what makes her holy.

Sometimes I think we imagine the people in Jesus's family tree as spiritual superheroes. But Ruth reminds us that God builds redemption not just through miracles but through mustard seeds—tiny, persistent acts of faith and love. God takes a foreign widow with nothing but her word and her willingness and grafts her into the very lineage of the Messiah.

In fact, Ruth is one of only five women named in Jesus's genealogy. Her story matters. Her loyalty matters. Her outsider status matters. In a season like Advent, where we often feel the tension between joy and sorrow, community and loneliness, Ruth reminds us that belonging isn't always inherited; it's sometimes chosen. And when we choose love, even when it costs us, we draw closer to the heart of Christ.

I love Ruth's connection to Rebekah, two women bound by their bold willingness to go where they felt called. Their deliberate decisions gave shape to God's work in the world, and through them, salvation has come to all. Ruth's great-grandson will be David. And generations after David will come Jesus, born in Bethlehem, the very town Ruth chose to make her home. Think about that. Her faithfulness didn't just bless Naomi. It prepared the soil for the Savior of the world.

That's what Advent is, in so many ways: the slow, faithful preparation of something beautiful. Not through big fanfare, but through small acts of loyalty and love. Through staying when we could leave. Through hoping when we feel empty. Through making room when our lives feel full.

Ruth didn't know where her story would lead when she said, "I will go." But God did.

So, this Advent, if you find yourself in a season of uncertainty, or if you're weary from doing good with little recognition, remember Ruth. Let her story strengthen your steps. Let her promise echo in your soul. And as you go through this season, let Ruth remind you that sometimes the most Christlike thing you can do is simply stay—with love, with faith, with God.

- Who has been a Ruth in your life? What difference did they make?
- When was the last time you thanked them for that? How can you do that today?
- How can God use you to be a Ruth for someone else? Who can you support boldly this week?

DAY 7

BOAZ

Then [Ruth] fell prostrate, with her face to the ground, and said to him, "Why have I found favor in your sight, that you should take notice of me, when I am a foreigner?" But Boaz answered her, "All that you have done for your mother-in-law since the death of your husband has been fully told me, how you left your father and mother and your native land and came to a people that you did not know before. May the LORD reward you for your deeds, and may you have a full reward from the LORD, the God of Israel, under whose wings you have come for refuge!"

Ruth 2:10-12

Boaz is a quiet kind of hero. His story in the Book of Ruth is understated but deeply impactful. He's introduced not with spectacle but with an insight into his character. He's described as a man of standing, a man of great wealth, but more important, *worthy*. A man of valor. A man of integrity. In Hebrew, the word used for Boaz in Ruth 2:1 is *gibbor hayil*, a term that describes not just physical strength or financial success but also moral courage and spiritual weight. He's the kind of man whose righteousness isn't loud, but it lasts.

We meet him in his field. He owns the land, but he pays close attention to those working on it. He notices Ruth right away, not just because she's new, but because he's the kind of man who *notices people.* He sees how hard she's working. He's heard about her story, how she left her homeland to care for Naomi, how she chose to follow Israel's God. And when he speaks to her, it's with kindness, blessing, and dignity.

That alone would've been something—a powerful Israelite landowner speaking directly to a Moabite widow with compassion and welcome. But Boaz goes further. He ensures Ruth's safety in the field. He instructs his workers to look out for her and even to leave behind extra grain for her to gather. He takes care of Ruth and Naomi without making a scene. He honors her without seeking credit.

And then, when Naomi sends Ruth to him in the dead of night, when she places herself at his feet, a humble and bold request for redemption, Boaz doesn't take advantage of her. He doesn't mock her or shame her. He blesses her again. And he sets out to do the honorable thing.

Boaz is a *redeemer.* Not just in title, but in action.

In ancient Israel, the role of the kinsman-redeemer (or *go'el*) was a legal and deeply spiritual responsibility. A redeemer was someone who stepped in to protect the vulnerable, to restore property, to continue a family line, and to ensure justice. This calling was traditional, but it wasn't mandatory. It could have been quite expensive and risky to act in this way. Boaz has a hundred reasons to walk away. Ruth's story was complicated. She came with baggage, loss, and cultural tension. But Boaz doesn't flinch. He says yes.

He says yes to redemption. He says yes to a future that includes Ruth. And in doing so, Boaz becomes part of the very family line that will lead to King David and, eventually, to Jesus.

There's something so beautiful about Boaz's kind of strength. It's not loud or performative. It's not rooted in dominance or bravado. It's rooted in faithfulness. In responsibility. In tenderness. His masculinity isn't toxic; it's redemptive. He's protective, not possessive. Generous, not self-promoting. He models what it looks like to hold power with grace.

I think of men like that I've known. A Sunday school teacher who always showed up early to make sure the coffee was hot. A father who took time to really listen, even when he didn't know what to say. A church member who always volunteered for the quiet jobs no one noticed, ushering, folding bulletins, fixing whatever needed fixing. Men who saw others clearly, who treated people with respect, no matter their past—people who made spaces feel safe. Boaz reminds me of them.

And Boaz reminds me that the Christmas story doesn't just depend on dramatic miracles; it depends on ordinary people doing faithful things. Just like Joseph will quietly choose to stay with Mary, just like the innkeeper will make room in a stable, Boaz makes space in his life for someone on the margins. And that's where the real redemption starts.

This is what Advent invites us into: the sacred, daily work of noticing others. Of showing up with integrity. Of choosing grace when the world expects something colder or harder. Advent isn't just about waiting; it's about becoming the kind of people who can carry God's promise with care.

Boaz didn't know that generations later, his name would be read aloud in churches around the globe. He didn't know that his faithfulness would echo all the way to Bethlehem. He just knew what was right, and he did it.

This season, may we learn from him. May we see the people on the margins. May we treat others with mercy. And may we never underestimate what God can do through steady faithfulness and quiet strength.

Because sometimes, the most powerful presence at the table is the one who simply showed up, made room, and said yes.

- How can you be better at noticing the needs and concerns of others?
- Have you ever felt like you had a kinsman-redeemer, someone who stood by you and had your back? How did that feel?
- How can you be that way for someone in your life this week?

DAY 8

JESSE

A shoot shall come out from the stump of Jesse,
and a branch shall grow out of his roots.
The spirit of the LORD shall rest on him,
the spirit of wisdom and understanding,
the spirit of counsel and might,
the spirit of knowledge and the fear of the LORD.
His delight shall be in the fear of the LORD.

He shall not judge by what his eyes see
or decide by what his ears hear,
but with righteousness he shall judge for the poor
and decide with equity for the oppressed of the earth;
he shall strike the earth with the rod of his mouth,
and with the breath of his lips he shall kill the wicked.

Isaiah 11:1-4

For many of us, the beauty and wonder of the Christmas season are about place as much as they are about anything else. Certain locations become sacred simply because of what happens there during this season. Some of these are places we only visit in December: the Christmas tree farm where laughter pierces the cold air, the light display on the downtown square that feels almost magical after dark, or the state capitol glowing against the winter sky. These places anchor our memories. They remind us that Christmas is not only something we believe but something we experience with our bodies, our senses, and our presence.

There are also places that exist year-round but are transformed during the Christmas season into something altogether different. I know this to be true of a particular room in my mother-in-law's home. It is the same house where my wife grew up—a warm, beautiful home nestled in a small town in Arkansas, full of history and family stories. Most of the year, when we visit, there is one room we rarely use: the music room. It is a lovely space but not a practical one. It is not designed for grandchildren to run through or for family to gather and linger. Inside sits a beautiful piano, carefully chosen antique furniture, and framed portraits of all three of her children on their wedding days. It is a room that invites admiration but not activity.

On most visits, there is simply no reason to go into that room. Life happens elsewhere, around the kitchen table where meals are shared or on the back patio where conversations stretch long into the evening. But at Christmas, everything changes. Each year, my mother-in-law places her Christmas tree in the music room. It is a real tree, decorated with care and intention, glowing with lights and ornaments that tell stories of years gone by. Suddenly, the room that is usually overlooked becomes the heart of the house. On Christmas, all the children and grandchildren gather there. Presents are opened, laughter fills the space, and joy spills into every corner. A room that once felt distant becomes full of life, love, and connection. The place that was often forgotten becomes sacred, simply because of what happens there.

Place mattered deeply in the first Christmas story as well. Jesus was not born just anywhere. He was born in Bethlehem, a small and seemingly insignificant town. *Bethlehem*, translated into English, means "the house of bread" or "the land of bread." It was farmland, ordinary land, worked by ordinary people. It was the place where Naomi and Ruth's family land was restored through the faithfulness and kindness of Boaz. It was the place where Ruth and Boaz's grandson would continue to work the fields and raise his family. That grandson's name was Jesse, the father of David.

Jesse is a name we do not usually linger on very long. His faithfulness is often overlooked, and his story is rarely told in detail. But the prophets remembered him. Again and again, they spoke of the "stump of Jesse," insisting that hope would spring from his line. Their commitment to naming Jesse should tell us something important. He represents the kind of faithfulness that does not seek recognition but creates space for God's work to unfold. He trusts in God in the big things and the small things. If his story was different, and his son didn't become king, his faith would have remained unchanged.

When the prophet Samuel travels to Bethlehem, he knows something Jesse does not—that God is about to choose a new king. Jesse only knows that Samuel has come to his home to anoint one of his sons for a special purpose. He does not imagine that the throne of Israel is at stake. Saul is still king. From Jesse's perspective, this is an act of service and trust, not ambition.

Some have been quick to criticize Jesse for presenting his oldest and strongest sons first, assuming he misunderstood God or lacked spiritual insight. I think that criticism is misplaced. Jesse was responding faithfully with the information he had. He brought forward sons who were capable, prepared, and willing to serve. That is not failure; that is good parenting and faithful stewardship. Jesse should be commended for raising sons ready to answer God's call, for being willing to release one of them from the family farm, and for listening attentively to God's voice through Samuel.

Here, in Bethlehem, an easily overlooked farming village, we find a man whose quiet obedience prepares the way for something extraordinary. Jesse does not become king. His name is rarely spoken aloud. And yet, without his faithfulness, David's story never begins. The greatest king Israel would ever know emerges from a home shaped by obedience, humility, and trust in God.

Sometimes we are quick to forget the people in our own lives whose deep faithfulness is overshadowed by those who stand in the spotlight. Jesse gets forgotten because David becomes the king after God's own heart, the warrior-poet who unites Israel and is ancestor to Christ. But David's greatness does not diminish his father's faithfulness. They are not in competition. Jesse's obedience creates the conditions for David's calling.

Jesse may never have expected to be the father of a king. He came from an unimportant place, lived an ordinary life, and worked common land. But he stayed faithful where he was. And when the moment came, he brought David forward. That faithfulness—quiet, unseen, and rooted in place—became part of God's salvation story.

Advent reminds us that God often chooses forgotten places and overlooked people to do his greatest work. Bethlehem mattered. Jesse mattered. The music room matters. And so do the places and people we may be tempted to overlook today. God delights in transforming ordinary spaces into holy ground and is still doing it today.

- Do you have preconceived notions about Jesse that could be reconsidered?
- Is there a person in your life whose steady faithfulness often goes unnoticed? How can you show them how much you appreciate their service to God and others?
- Jesse faithfully raised his family, without expectations of power or prestige. How can you seek a deeper faithfulness without expectations about rewards or benefits?

DAY 9

DAVID

It was told King David, "The LORD has blessed the household of Obed-edom and all that belongs to him because of the ark of God." So David went and brought up the ark of God from the house of Obed-edom to the city of David with rejoicing, and when those who bore the ark of the LORD had gone six paces, he sacrificed an ox and a fatted calf. David danced before the LORD with all his might; David was girded with a linen ephod. So David and all the house of Israel brought up the ark of the LORD with shouting and with the sound of the trumpet.

2 Samuel 6:12-15

Jesus's connection to King David is of the highest importance because the life of David forms a bridge between the kingdom of Israel and the kingdom of heaven. We might ask why the Gospels go to such great lengths to trace Jesus's genealogy back to David. They are not merely offering historical detail; they are proclaiming fulfillment. Fulfillment of prophecies, of course, and also fulfillment of the covenant God made with David during his reign. God promised David that his throne would be established forever, and in Jesus Christ, that promise finds its ultimate and eternal expression. David's kingdom was real and powerful, but it was also temporary. Jesus's kingdom is unseen yet unshakable, rooted not in military strength or political dominance but in righteousness, grace, and sacrificial love.

David is often remembered as the king after God's own heart, and for good reason. His faith is legendary—the shepherd boy who stood before Goliath with nothing but a sling and unshakable trust in God, who left the valley victoriously in the name of God. His leadership reunited the tribes of Israel and restored Jerusalem as the heart of the nation.

And in today's passage, we see David at one of his finest moments: rejoicing as the ark of the covenant is brought home. The ark represented the very presence of God among the people. Its return signaled more than a military victory over the Philistines—it was a spiritual restoration for Israel. God was once again at the center.

And yet, David's story, much like his ancestor Judah's, is not one of uninterrupted faithfulness. He is also the king who failed spectacularly, abused his power, orchestrated the death of Uriah, and took Bathsheba as his own. Scripture does not sanitize David's story, and that honesty matters. David was deeply loved by God, but he was also deeply flawed. His life reminds us that even the most faithful servants of God remain human, capable of sin, regret, and brokenness. David's repentance was real, but so were the consequences of his actions.

This is where Jesus stands in sharp and beautiful contrast. Jesus is the king that David could never be. Where David's reign was marred by sin, Jesus's life was without blemish. Where David's obedience wavered, Jesus's obedience was complete, even to the point of death on a cross. David points us forward, but Jesus fulfills what David only foreshadowed.

Still, when I think of David, I often return to this scene in 2 Samuel 6: David dancing before the Lord with all his might. Not calculating how he appears. Not concerned with maintaining royal dignity. Not guarding his reputation. He dances because God is present. He dances because the ark is returning. He dances because joy that surpasses all understanding has come to live in his heart.

In this moment, David isn't showing off his military prowess or superior faithfulness. This is worship, fully open and expressed. We see that David lays aside his royal robes and wears a simple linen ephod, which is the garment of a priest. David isn't asking God to recognize his own greatness but comes as a grateful worshiper responding to God's grace and leadership. Later in the chapter, when Michal criticizes him for embarrassing himself, David responds with words that still challenge us today: "I will make myself yet more contemptible than this, and I will be humbled in my own eyes" (6:22). In other words, David is willing to look foolish if it means honoring God.

There is something that speaks deeply to Advent in David's attitude. While society tells us that in December we have to have perfect decorations and all the right gifts and check off all the boxes of our traditions, Advent invites us to loosen our grip on appearances, expectations, and control. It reminds us that God often enters our lives in ways that disrupt our sense of order. A pregnancy announcement to a young virgin. A baby in a manger. Shepherds instead of priests. A Savior born not into wealth or power but into vulnerability. The kingdom of God rarely arrives with polish. It arrives with wonder.

This scene also reminds me of one of my favorite Christmas songs, "It's Christmas, So Who Cares" by Andrew Galucki. The song captures the messy beauty of the season with lines of deep honesty: "The lights are flickerin', the family is bickerin', the candle wick is burning down, but it's still Christmas somehow."

"It's still Christmas, somehow." That is the heart of David's dance. It is worship that refuses to wait for perfection. It is joy that breaks through disorder. It is gratitude that rises even when circumstances aren't what we had hoped for and expectations are unmet. David dances in the chaos of noise, movement, trumpets, and shouting. And God delights in it.

As we approach the final days before Christmas, the pressure to get everything right can feel overwhelming. Gifts to buy. Meals to prepare. Schedules to coordinate. Traditions to uphold. Expectations to meet. It is easy to lose sight of why we are doing any of it in the first place. We can become so focused on creating the "perfect" Christmas that we miss the presence of Christ altogether.

But, friends, Advent calls us back. It calls us to remember a lord-a-leaping, if you will, David dancing in praise. A man who understood that God's presence was worth more than dignity, more than control, more than the approval of others. David reminds us that worship is not about having everything together; it is about fully offering ourselves to God.

So in these last few days before Christmas, I invite you to slow down. Linger when you look at the lights. Let the glow remind you that the light has come into the world. Hug your family tightly, even in the middle of the mess. Savor the food, the laughter, the quiet moments, and even the imperfections. Let gratitude drown out your anxiety. Let joy interrupt your stress. Maybe, just maybe, you could do a little dancing.

And above all, let every part of this season, every decoration, every song, every shared meal, point you back to the incredible goodness of God—the God who kept his promise to David. The God who sent his Son through David's line. The God who still meets us, not in perfection, but in presence. Like David, may we worship with all our might, and may our joy bear witness to the king who has come and is coming again.

- Have you ever felt like David does here, wanting to celebrate with God?
- What part of the celebration of Christmas are you anticipating most?
- How can you focus less on the stress of "doing Christmas" and focus more on the gift of celebrating God in Christmas?

DAY 10

SOLOMON

"But will God indeed dwell on the earth? Even heaven, and the highest heaven cannot contain you, much less this house that I have built! Regard your servant's prayer and his plea, O Lord my God, heeding the cry and the prayer that your servant prays to you today, that your eyes may be open night and day toward this house, the place of which you said, 'My name shall be there,' that you may heed the prayer that your servant prays toward this place. Hear the plea of your servant and of your people Israel when they pray toward this place; O hear in heaven your dwelling place; hear and forgive."

1 Kings 8:27-30

Have you ever experienced something so powerful, so marvelous, so meaningful that you needed a minute to reflect so you could fully understand what was happening around you? Maybe it was during a big game, when a player displayed unbelievable athleticism. Perhaps it was a concert when a musician or band seemed transcendent. I know I feel this way whenever I encounter a true expert in their field, someone whose years of training and experience are brought to bear in sheer excellence. I have been blown away by the voice of an incredible singer and the music that flows from a violin played by a concertmaster. I have been moved by the work of a chef, perfectly balancing flavors and textures. I have also been deeply moved by the work of someone skillfully working the land with an excavator or the planning and construction of a skyscraper.

I will never forget a moment like this when I was a young pastor in one of my first appointments. Our church was growing and thriving, and we needed more room to park. A deeply faithful member of our congregation lived next door to the parsonage, which was directly across the street from the church. These members decided to leave their home and land to the church in their will for the church to use as it saw fit. It was the perfect place for us to spread out and increase our parking, but to do so, we had to move the house that was on the land. Instead of tearing the home down, a company specializing in moving homes came in and we struck a deal. If they would move the home off the land, we would sell them the home for $1.

Watching the crew come in with special jacks and cranes to meticulously lift the home off of its piers was breathtaking. Seeing a structure so large and so heavy moved with great care displayed their skill and craftsmanship. This moment of excellence from blue-collar workers in jeans and hard hats was surprising and exceptional. When you take a moment to reflect on all the years of training, failing, learning, striving, and growing that go into any moment of excellence, it can take your breath away. Ultimately, these moments leave us asking, How? How do they do it? How does someone get that skilled? How could I ever do something like that?

These questions remind me of the one Solomon asks as he opens his prayer of dedication for the temple of God that he has just built. In the pages preceding our reading for today, we see almost three chapters describing Solomon's wisdom and his desire to build a temple where God can dwell among the people. We see the painstaking detail that is put into its construction and how Solomon desires to create a place for God to be with the people and the people to have access to God. When construction is finished, Solomon gathers all of Israel in Jerusalem and consecrates the temple to God. The ark of the covenant, the relic from the time of Moses and a signpost of God's faithfulness, is brought into the inner sanctum of the temple. The presence of God in the form of a cloud of smoke so powerfully fills the room, it forces everyone inside to leave. God's presence in this form harkens us back to God leading the Israelites out of their slavery in Egypt by a cloud in the daytime. God's presence was with them in the wilderness, and God's presence is with them now in the temple.

What I really love about this story, though, is that Solomon—the man who asked God for incredible wisdom, who some say was the wisest man to ever live—begins his prayer of dedication with a question: "But will God indeed dwell on the earth?" (8:27). It's a question like those we ask when we experience the exceptional moments. Solomon is essentially saying to God, "Is this for real? Are you really going to be with us this powerfully and clearly?" It is almost as if Solomon finds everything that he has just witnessed with his own eyes hard to believe. The wisest man in all the world has no words to offer. He needs a moment to grasp the fullness of the beauty he has just experienced.

I think that is the point of Advent; it's why we are given these four weeks to wait and prepare for the moment when God really dwells on the earth. We need this time to reflect on the miraculous gift that is the presence of God with us now and always. It isn't something we can comprehend in just one day. It causes us to step back and marvel at the excellent goodness of a God who comes to save and redeem.

One of my favorite hymns is "And Can It Be, That I Should Gain?" by Charles Wesley, the brother of John Wesley. It is a hymn that asks a question like the one Solomon asked, like the ones we ask:

> Amazing love! how can it be
> That Thou, my God, shouldst die for me? . . .

He left His Father's throne above,
So free, so infinite His grace;
Emptied Himself of all but love,
And bled for Adam's helpless race:
'Tis mercy all, immense and free;
For, O my God, it found out me.

The busyness of the holiday season often rushes us to Christmas, the big day with the presents and food, family and friends. Advent, though, calls us to slow down and marvel, wonder and reflect, and ultimately have our breath taken away. Ask the questions: How can it be? Will God really dwell on earth? Are you really this good, God? Ask them and allow this time in Advent to be the space and place in which God answers them.

- When have you experienced excellence that stopped you in your tracks?
- Have you ever asked a Solomon-sized question of God? Did you give yourself time to really listen to God's answer?
- How can you take the season of Advent as a time to slowly unravel the good news of Christ's arrival in your life?

DAY 11

ZERUBBABEL

Jeshua son of Jozadak with his fellow priests and Zerubbabel son of Shealtiel with his kin set out to build the altar of the God of Israel, to offer burnt offerings on it, as prescribed in the law of Moses the man of God. They set up the altar on its foundation because they were in dread of the peoples of the lands, and they offered burnt offerings upon it to the Lord*, morning and evening. . . . From the first day of the seventh month they began to offer burnt offerings to the* Lord*. But the foundation of the temple of the* Lord *was not yet laid. So they gave money to the masons and the carpenters, and food, drink, and oil to the Sidonians and the Tyrians to bring cedar trees from Lebanon to the sea, to Joppa, according to the grant that they had from King Cyrus of Persia.*

Ezra 3:2-3, 6-7

Zerubbabel is one of the descendants of Jesus we tend to know the least about, and he is also one of the last figures in Scripture who stands clearly within Jesus's family line. He does not receive the narrative attention given to Abraham or David, nor does his story come wrapped in the dramatic twists of Ruth or Rahab. There are no epic battles attached to his name, no miraculous escapes, and no poetic psalms attributed to him. And yet, Zerubbabel's place in the story of God's people is far more important than his relative obscurity might suggest.

Zerubbabel is like that unassuming cousin who never demands the spotlight at the family dinner table. He does not arrive in flashy clothes or talk about his impressive achievements. He listens more than he speaks. He asks good questions. He helps clear the dishes when no one is looking. My wife, Mary, and I each have a cousin like this. You would never guess at first glance that both of them are incredibly intelligent, high-performing in their respective fields, and deeply successful in everything they do. Their strength is not loud. Their confidence does not require attention. They simply show up, do the work in front of them, and make life better for everyone around them.

That is very much the spirit of Zerubbabel.

Zerubbabel emerges in Scripture at a moment when Israel is exhausted, disoriented, and unsure of its future. The people have lived in exile in Babylon for decades. They have lost their land, their temple, and the rhythms of worship that once defined them. When permission is finally granted for the Israelites to return home, the journey is not triumphant. There is no grand parade. What awaits them in Jerusalem is rubble, broken walls, and memories of what once was. Hope feels fragile. I compare this journey to the one the Hebrews made when they fled Egypt. During that journey, they were unsure of what lay ahead but incredibly hopeful for a land to make their own. Yet now they are returning to the destroyed remains of what had been. I cannot imagine this mixture of excitement to be free mixed with despair at what that freedom meant.

Zerubbabel steps into this moment as the lay leader of the first wave of Israelites returning from exile. He is not a priest. He is not a prophet. He is a governor, a civic leader tasked with organizing a discouraged people. Alongside him is Jeshua the priest, and together they take on the daunting work of rebuilding the temple and restoring the spiritual life of the nation. It is not glamorous work. It is slow, expensive, and filled with opposition. The people are tempted to focus on rebuilding their own homes first, to secure their own comfort before attending to God's house.

But Zerubbabel understands something essential: The temple must come first. Rebuilding the temple is not about architecture or nostalgia. This is a statement of faith. It is a public declaration that God still dwells among God's people. It is a visible sign that despite exile, loss, and suffering, the covenant remains. God has not abandoned them. Their identity is still rooted in worship.

Through the prophets Haggai and Zechariah, God speaks directly to Zerubbabel. Again and again, the message is one of encouragement. God instructs Zerubbabel to do the small things well, for little is much when God is involved. The foundation being laid may not look impressive, especially compared to Solomon's temple, but faithfulness is not measured by the human regard for size and splendor. God reminds Zerubbabel that this rebuilding will not happen by might or by power but by God's spirit. Zerubbabel's leadership is not about force or charisma; it is about perseverance, trust, and obedience.

Advent is a season that teaches us to value beginnings that feel small. A pregnancy announcement to an unwed teenager. A baby in a manger. A people returning home with more memories than resources. A foundation laid before walls are raised. Zerubbabel stands in that space between promise and fulfillment. He does not see the finished story. He simply does the faithful work of preparing the way.

As we sit in this season, many of us carry a complicated mix of emotions. Christmas can be the very best time of the year, bringing genuine joy, traditions we cherish, gatherings with family and friends, and food that nourishes both body and soul. There is laughter and music and warmth. But there is also stress. Financial strain from gift-giving. Exhaustion from travel. The emotional weight of complicated family dynamics. And beneath it all, grief. Loved ones who are no longer at the table. Relationships that have changed or faded over time.

Zerubbabel's story reminds us that God meets us in the middle of all of it. Not after the mess is cleaned up. Not once everything is resolved. God meets his people while the city is still in ruins. He calls them to faithfulness not because life is easy but because God is present. Jesus, born into Zerubbabel's family line, is the ultimate expression of that truth. *Emmanuel*—God with us—means God is present in both joy and grief, celebration and sorrow, hope and uncertainty.

There is a quiet strength in choosing to put God first when everything else feels unsettled. Zerubbabel could have focused solely on making life easier for himself and the returning exiles. Instead, he prioritized worship. He trusted that rebuilding the temple would re-center the people, reminding them who they were and whose they were. In doing so, he helped prepare the way for generations to come—including Jesus himself.

As we gather around our tables and trees, our own "house" feels full. Over these weeks, we have welcomed the ancestors of Jesus into our Advent journey. We have listened to their stories, learned from their faithfulness, and seen how God works through both the extraordinary and the ordinary. Zerubbabel's presence among them reminds us that significance is not always loud or dramatic. Sometimes it looks like steady obedience, faithful leadership, and the courage to begin again.

As we move through these holy days, may we learn from Zerubbabel to put God first in all we do. Embrace every aspect of this season—the joy, the sorrow, the memories, and the hope. Praise God for all the good it brings, and trust that even the quiet work you are doing now is part of a much larger story God is still writing.

- How can you put God first in your life over the next few days?
- Is your heart ready to receive Jesus? Have you made room for him at the table?
- What small things can you do in your life to prepare for the Lord?

DAY 12

ZECHARIAH

Zechariah was filled with the Holy Spirit and prophesied:

"Blessed be the Lord God of Israel,
for he has looked favorably on his people and redeemed them.
He has raised up a mighty savior for us
in the house of his child David,
as he spoke through the mouth of his holy prophets from of old,
that we would be saved from our enemies and from the hand of all who hate us.
Thus he has shown the mercy promised to our ancestors
and has remembered his holy covenant,
the oath that he swore to our ancestor Abraham,
to grant us that we, being rescued from the hands of our enemies,
might serve him without fear, in holiness and righteousness
in his presence all our days."

Luke 1:67-75

For as long as I can remember, Zechariah's name has been dragged through the mud. His bad reputation comes particularly in comparison to his wife and her reception of the divine good news of their coming child. Elizabeth, who so readily accepted the birth announcement, is lifted up for her powerful faith, while Zechariah gets chastised for his understandable incredulousness when Gabriel approaches him in the temple. I understand it; Gabriel did seem to be upset with Zechariah and took away his ability to speak for the duration of the pregnancy. We like things to be binary, black and white, easy to understand. So we lift up Elizabeth and make Zechariah the foil to her faith.

That isn't fair, though, and treating him this way robs him of the respect he is due, and it robs us of a powerful character who fills a very important role in the story of Jesus. Luke describes Zechariah as a priest in the line of Aaron who, along with his wife, lived blamelessly before God. Zechariah was an upright and faithful priest, and at the time, this wasn't the only possibility. There are suggestions in the New Testament and elsewhere that corruption had become part of the religious establishment. Zechariah isn't part of this, though; he is from the right family line, and he takes his duties seriously.

It is while performing those duties that he is met by Gabriel and hears that God has answered his prayer: They will have a child. Incredulous, Zechariah asks how this can be. This question matters deeply. For in it, Zechariah is building the first pillar on the bridge that will span the gap between God's promise to Abraham so many years ago and its fulfillment in the coming Christ Child. His response to the angel reminds us of Abraham's response when he hears that he and Sarah will have a child, and that their descendants will outnumber the stars. Again, it is not a condemning lack of faith, but a sincere concern about how God can do what God has promised. This connection between Abraham and Zechariah begins the chasm-spanning pathway that is the fulfillment of God's salvation covenant.

Zechariah reminds me of those family members we have who intentionally and with great effort maintain the family's connection to their ancestors, their traditions, their stories, and their legacy. At Christmas they tell the stories of the best gifts, funniest mix-ups, and meaningful moments. They keep the memories of ancestors long gone for the new generations and share the traditions that unite the family. I have an uncle who is this way. Not only does he keep the memories of our family alive but he also helps ground our family in the truth of our not-so-distant past—a past mired by hardship and struggle, poverty and war. It is important that my children, who are growing up very differently, understand that their ancestors fought and sacrificed to help them live as bountifully as they do now. It is important that we keep this bridge between the past and future strong.

Just as Zechariah's question to Gabriel is the first step in the bridge, his song found in our reading for today is the last one. His first words after nine months of silence connect the dots between what God promised Abraham and what God is doing in the life of his son, John. This connection between God's promises of old and their fulfillment in John and Jesus is of utmost importance. Jesus's story doesn't happen in a vacuum; it takes place in the midst of the much longer narrative of God's activity with Israel and, in turn, humanity. Without Zechariah, we might not see that so clearly.

So I hope you will join me in restoring Zechariah's reputation. He faithfully helped the people then and helps us today to connect the dots in God's salvation story. Just like our relatives who are the keepers of family history, Zechariah places Jesus in the light of God's desire to redeem and restore all of creation unto God.

- Who is the keeper of your family history? Can you become the keeper of God's story inside your family, so you can tell the stories of God's activity in your lives?
- What do you think about Zechariah as the bridge between Abraham's covenant and the coming Messiah? Why might it be important to connect to the Jewish or Israelite origins of Christianity?
- How can you be more prepared to receive what you have prayed for than Zechariah was?

DAY 13

ELIZABETH

In those days Mary set out and went with haste to a Judean town in the hill country, where she entered the house of Zechariah and greeted Elizabeth. When Elizabeth heard Mary's greeting, the child leaped in her womb. And Elizabeth was filled with the Holy Spirit and exclaimed with a loud cry, "Blessed are you among women, and blessed is the fruit of your womb. And why has this happened to me, that the mother of my Lord comes to me? For as soon as I heard the sound of your greeting, the child in my womb leaped for joy. And blessed is she who believed that there would be a fulfillment of what was spoken to her by the Lord."

Luke 1:39-45

It is hard to talk about Advent, waiting, and expecting baby Jesus without thinking about pregnancy. It is interesting to me how these two notions got mixed up together. Why do we use the terms "expecting" or "expectant" as a polite way to speak about someone who is pregnant? It turns out that these words have been used with this meaning in the English language since the early 1800s and first were used to describe just the father, who of course isn't actually carrying the baby. But since then, the terms have been applied to both men and women.

The words give us the idea of looking hopefully into the future, thinking about all of the good that lies in wait for us. It is a blessing to be able to look forward, not with fear and anxiety, but with excitement. And when we dive into the character we are looking at today, I think that pretty perfectly sums up her time as a pregnant woman. She was in this blessed state of great expectation, and she used that to be a blessing to others and the world. I am not talking about the mother of Jesus but rather Elizabeth.

Luke describes Elizabeth as a righteous and faithful woman, the wife of a priest, who has been unable to have children. Now an older woman, beyond typical childbearing years, it appears as though her future was set. In this culture, it was a primary role of the wife to bear children, and so Elizabeth must have lived her days with shame and a sense of failure at her most core responsibility. But like other faithful, childless women in Scripture, her faith never wavers, and she finds that she is pregnant with a special child as a result of God's mighty work. What Elizabeth really models for us is a patient faithfulness.

First, we see that Elizabeth's patient faithfulness allowed her to have hopeful expectations. The way that Elizabeth was able to hold on to her faith in the face of incredibly difficult circumstances. Where most would get angry with God, blame God for their problems, or simply lose faith in God's ability to act, Elizabeth did none of those things. She simply held on to her righteousness and a belief that God would bless her. But it is clear that while she didn't necessarily expect God to bless her with a pregnancy, she wasn't pigeonholing the role God could take in her life. Instead, she had a patient faith that allowed God to work however God saw fit.

This patient faithfulness is difficult for us who live in a microwave culture. We want our calling and our blessing and we want them right now. We want our prayers to be answered, the way we want them to be answered, as soon as we offer them. But patient faithfulness like Elizabeth's allows us to wait for God to bring us what is right in the right time—not our time. This patient faithfulness could help all of us build our own faithful expectations not only of the Christmas season but all of our lives, leading us to the understanding that God has both great blessings and great work for us to do, in God's own time and way.

We see that this patient faithfulness allowed Elizabeth to be filled with the Holy Spirit. In a dramatic movement, when Mary and Elizabeth are together, Elizabeth is flooded with the power of the Holy Spirit of God and shouts out a powerful prophecy herself. It is in this spirit that she sees that Mary is pregnant, and she also is the first person to acknowledge that Mary's child is the Lord, God incarnate. Elizabeth's faithfulness allowed her to serve as a vessel of the Holy Spirit who brings awareness to what God is doing here. She is able to identify to Mary, to herself, and to all the world that these two pregnancies are not just miraculous in and of themselves, but that God is working out redemption for all people through the fruit of their wombs. We are called to this kind of faithfulness, wherein our words are the cry of the Holy Spirit, pointing out to the world what God is doing and how God is doing it.

I am reminded of the patient faithfulness of a man who had lost his job and felt as if his life was falling apart. When he had nothing to cling to, he turned to God. For the first time, he truly relied upon God. For over a year, he struggled but also knew that God was working in and through him. All the while, he began to be a witness to others about God's love and activity. He saw God's presence in a new way and was able to lead others to see it as well.

But Elizabeth impresses me most when she goes against social expectations. Many people would have shamed Mary, dressed her down for becoming pregnant before marriage. Society said that Elizabeth should have denied Mary's joy in her pregnancy and sent her back to her home. But Elizabeth did none of that, because through the wisdom of the Holy Spirit, she recognized that God was at work. And so instead of shaming Mary, Elizabeth pronounced a blessing over her.

Instead of rejecting her, Elizabeth brought her into her home for three months. Instead of denying her joy, Elizabeth celebrated with Mary, because she saw God's hand moving, God doing something wonderful, God working miracles all over the place.

But we don't need that special spiritual vision of Elizabeth to be able to see God at work. Where might God be at work in our lives through people whom we might not anticipate or society might even reject? We need to turn our eyes to the outsider, the outcast, the shamed, and the forgotten, because as we see over and again in Scripture, God works in ways we often do not expect. We need to be like Elizabeth and have a patient faith that expects God to do great and wonderful things without deciding when and how these things should happen. Instead, with open hearts and hands, we watch and see what God will do and join in.

- Do you find it a struggle to live out patient faithfulness? When is it the most difficult?
- How can you be a vessel of the Holy Spirit's voice and pour it out into the world this week?
- Where is God calling you to go against what is popular or expected in order to build the Kingdom?

DAY 14

JOHN THE BAPTIST

The word of God came to John son of Zechariah in the wilderness. He went into all the region around the Jordan, proclaiming a baptism of repentance for the forgiveness of sins, as it is written in the book of the words of the prophet Isaiah,

"The voice of one crying out in the wilderness:
'Prepare the way of the Lord;
make his paths straight.
Every valley shall be filled,
and every mountain and hill shall be made low,
and the crooked shall be made straight,
and the rough ways made smooth,
and all flesh shall see the salvation of God.'"

Luke 3:2-6

The wilderness. Oh, the wilderness. Throughout Scripture we see stories of God's people in the wilderness. The word describes the dangerous, untamed desert, which is the opposite of good, fertile land that we see, for example, in the garden in Genesis. From the very beginning, we see God taming the wilderness and placing a garden in the midst of it. But when Adam and Eve fail to live obediently there, they are forced out into the wilderness.

We see that people end up in the wilderness either because of their own doing, like Moses fleeing Egypt after murdering an Egyptian who was beating Israelites. But they can also end up there because of someone else, like David finding safety in the wilderness as he hides from a vengeful King Saul. In each case, God meets people in the wilderness to provide for their needs and often prepares them for some special calling or purpose. The wilderness is also a place of preparation, where the people of God learn to trust and listen to God and stay connected to God. Thus, the wilderness, a place of hardship and struggle, becomes a place where God refines and restores the people and prepares them to return to the garden once again.

With all this in mind, we hear the story of John the Baptist with a new spirit. Not just the wild man wearing animal skins and eating bugs, but a part of this long story of God's people in the wilderness. John, the son of a priest, is living in the time immediately following the Hasmonean dynasty, in which the priesthood had been corrupted. These leaders who freed Israel from Greek rule used the priesthood as a source of political power, and these roles were often given to the highest bidder.

As a result, a sect of devout Jews, led by a small group of priests, moved out into the wilderness around Jerusalem and established their more strict and traditional version of Judaism. These men and women were known as Essenes, and they sought to bring Israel back to faithfulness and obedience. Many scholars have pointed out the connections between the Essenes and John the Baptist, thus explaining his arrival from the wilderness, the draw that people in Jerusalem might have felt toward his message, and his teachings about repentance and baptism.

John was the voice from the wilderness bringing a message of refining and repentance to the people, the very things the wilderness has tended to impart throughout the Bible. If we were to read all of Luke 3, we would see that his message is one of justice, obedience, and personal faith. He is describing how the people of God can live in the garden of God once again, through repentance and obedience.

His message is ultimately one of hope—hope in a future lived inside the presence of God in the garden God created for us. In our reading for today, we see Luke quote from the prophecy found in Isaiah 40 about a voice crying out in the wilderness. This passage was originally uttered to a people living in exile, the wilderness, promising them that they were soon to return back to the land of Israel, the garden. The exiles' lives were being restored thanks to the goodness and kindness of God.

The connection is clear: John is the voice pointing us to a future in which we can leave the wilderness of sin and death and enter into the garden of abundant and eternal life. But his message wasn't gentle, and it wasn't well received, especially by those who needed to hear it the most.

Isn't that the way it is with truth tellers, though? My aunt Pat was that way. She didn't say anything that wasn't true and wouldn't hold back the truth to save feelings or practice Southern graces. I will never forget the time we gathered at the beach for our annual family vacation, and Pat gave me some truth I didn't want to hear. You see, I was in the middle of seminary, a full-time student working at a church as well. Mary and I were newly married, happy as could be. As a result of these factors, I had added a couple of unwanted pounds around my midsection, and their addition was painfully clear when swimming at the beach. Pat wasted no time in telling me that I had gained weight and needed to watch my health. Harsh, to be sure. True, absolutely. Pat's concern wasn't about my looks but my health. And because she wanted the best for me, she told me the truth. Aunt Pat was smart as a whip, had experienced great pain, and yet held on to an abiding faithfulness.

I think of Pat when I hear the message of John the Baptist. He pulled no punches and minced no words, but he was the voice from the place of refining and repentance, calling people to grab ahold of the life that really is life. His voice prepared the people for their Savior. God was once again using the wilderness as a place to draw people back into God's garden, once and for all, through Jesus Christ.

- Have you had an experience in the wilderness—a time of difficulty—that ultimately helped you trust in God's presence?
- How can the wilderness you experience lead you to repentance and renewal? Are you open to God's work in your life?
- Who are the truth tellers in your life, the people you have invited to speak deeply to your heart and walk with God? If you don't have any, how can you cultivate those relationships to grow in your faith?

DAY 15

GABRIEL

In the sixth month the angel Gabriel was sent by God to a town in Galilee called Nazareth, to a virgin engaged to a man whose name was Joseph, of the house of David. The virgin's name was Mary. And he came to her and said, "Greetings, favored one! The Lord is with you." But she was much perplexed by his words and pondered what sort of greeting this might be. The angel said to her, "Do not be afraid, Mary, for you have found favor with God. And now, you will conceive in your womb and bear a son, and you will name him Jesus. He will be great and will be called the Son of the Most High, and the Lord God will give to him the throne of his ancestor David. He will reign over the house of Jacob forever, and of his kingdom there will be no end."

Luke 1:26-33

I think every family has this person, the one who gathers and distributes information, the messenger, if you will. When a long-lost cousin graduates from college, it's the messenger's job to let everyone know. When someone gets engaged, diagnosed, promoted; or hospitalized, the messenger is the one who makes sure the news travels. They keep the group email chain alive or the family text thread updated with the latest developments, both joyful and heartbreaking.

My mother-in-law does this beautifully. She keeps her children connected to what is happening in the wider family, even when geography and time create distance. I'll admit, there are moments when I have to lean over and ask my wife to clarify who she's talking about, because some of these relatives are so far removed that I've never met them. And yet, the news is still shared. The connection still matters. The relationship is worth keeping alive.

That matters more than we realize. Because my side of the family doesn't really have one of those messengers anymore. My mother often filled that role, but since her passing, the connections don't feel as strong. I am at least partly to blame, as I haven't taken on the mantle from my mom and rebuilt those connections she fostered. Without a messenger, families can drift apart without even realizing it. The messenger plays a vital role in holding people together, reminding us that we belong to one another, sharing love, and announcing good news.

Angels, in Scripture, serve a similar purpose. They are messengers who bear God's word, carriers of divine announcements, bridges between heaven and earth. And among all the angels named in Scripture, Gabriel stands out as one of the most important messengers of good news. We most often associate Gabriel with Mary and the announcement of Jesus's birth, but that is not the first time Gabriel appears in the story of God's people.

We first encounter Gabriel in the Book of Daniel, during the Babylonian exile. Israel is living far from home, scattered and broken as a result of its unfaithfulness. In Daniel chapters 8 and 9, Gabriel appears twice. In the first encounter, Gabriel helps Daniel understand a troubling vision, acting as a translator between God's revelation and human understanding. Gabriel does not create the message; he clarifies it. He helps Daniel see what God is doing when the meaning feels overwhelming or unclear.

The second interaction is even more striking. In Daniel 9, Daniel prays one of the most honest and humble prayers in all of Scripture. He confesses the sins of the people. He names their failures without excuse. He pleads for mercy, not because Israel deserves it, but because God is gracious. Daniel's prayer is filled with repentance and longing. Gabriel appears to Daniel as this prayer ends.

Gabriel comes with good news. The exile will not last forever. God has heard the prayers of the people. Forgiveness has been granted. Restoration is coming. God is drawing near again, not to punish, but to save and redeem. In that moment, Gabriel becomes the announcer of salvation, the messenger who carries hope into a season of despair.

That moment in Daniel's story points directly forward to Gabriel's appearance to Mary. Once again, God's people are living under oppression. Once again, they are waiting for deliverance. Once again, God responds not with silence but with a message. Gabriel appears to a young girl in an ordinary place and announces that God is coming near, fully and forever. God will save His people not just from exile but from sin and death itself.

In both moments, Gabriel stands in the space between heaven and earth. He simply delivers news faithfully. Gabriel is the family messenger of God's people, reminding them that they are not forgotten, not abandoned, and not beyond redemption. God is still speaking. God is still acting. God is still near.

I think our world desperately needs more messengers of good news. We live in a time when bad news travels fast and hope feels fragile. We are constantly updated on everything that is broken, divided, and painful. What we need are people willing to carry a different kind of message. People willing to make the connections, to keep relationships strong, to remind others that they are seen and loved.

You and I are called to take up that role. We may not appear with wings or speak with angelic authority, but we are still people who have been sent, people with a message. We are still carriers of good news. We are bridges between God's love and a hurting world. That calling often looks far more ordinary than we expect. It looks like sending the text, making the call, writing the email. Showing up, checking in, refusing to let relationships fade into silence.

It also looks like sharing the deeper good news that God has drawn near in Jesus Christ. It is the truth that restoration is possible and forgiveness is accessible. That exile—whether spiritual, emotional, or relational—does not get the final word. When we speak words of hope, grace, and truth, we participate in the same work Gabriel began centuries ago.

As we gather around our trees and tables this Advent season, may we remember the power of the messenger. May we be people who carry good news into weary spaces. May we help hold families, friendships, and communities together through love and communication. And may we never forget that the greatest message we have to share is this: God is near, God saves, and God's love still binds us together.

- Gabriel's first words to Mary are "Greetings favored one, the Lord is with you." How would you feel to hear that message? How can you share it with others?
- Who is the messenger in your family, and have you thanked them for that work? How can you step into that role?
- How can you be a messenger for Christ this week?

DAY 16

MARY

Mary said to the angel, "How can this be, since I am a virgin?" The angel said to her, "The Holy Spirit will come upon you, and the power of the Most High will overshadow you; therefore the child to be born will be holy; he will be called Son of God. And now, your relative Elizabeth in her old age has also conceived a son, and this is the sixth month for her who was said to be barren. For nothing will be impossible with God." Then Mary said, "Here am I, the servant of the Lord; let it be with me according to your word." Then the angel departed from her.

Luke 1:34-38

I don't think there is a single season of the year that comes with the same kind of great expectations that surround the Christmas season. Sure, we all have expectations about the beauty of spring, the outdoor fun of the summer, or maybe the thrill of the hunt in the fall. But none of these compare to the expectations that surround Christmas.

Take a moment and think about all of the expectations you have this year or have had in the past. I know that there have been years in which I had high expectations for the gifts I was going to receive, and of course these expectations were not met because they weren't realistic. When they weren't met, my disappointment led to me to acting like a spoiled jerk, which I deeply regret. I know we often have lofty expectations about the food or the company, hoping to emulate years past. But almost more than anything else, we set these expectations for how we are going to feel, hoping that the Christmas spirit will take over and we will feel the magic of Christmas like we did when we were kids.

But the problem with expectations is that usually they are built on a shoddy foundation. We either set up our expectations on pride or we construct them on distorted images of the past. We build these hopes that our Christmas will be like the ones we used to have, but the problem is that those Christmases probably weren't as great as we remember them. There were stresses and issues, fights and budgets, burned turkeys and dry hams. But we forget all of that and just remember the best parts and then set expectations based on these perfect memories. The great expectations set us up for failure, for disappointment, and for heartache. But without them, we feel like we are without a plan or a purpose.

In the same way that we can misremember the Christmas seasons of old, we can also forget the reality of Mary, who she was and the deep faithfulness she displayed. As we look at Mary's life, we often forget the real details of who she was. Mary was, by every worldly measure, a nobody from nowhere. She came from Nazareth—a town that was small and insignificant enough that the earliest mention we have of it today is in the Gospels. As an unwed young woman, she had no real social standing, no wealth, no influence. In the first-century world, girls were considered of marriageable age around puberty. Many girls were engaged by the age of thirteen, while boys tended to be a bit older than that. Thus, by our modern understanding, Mary was likely around the age of a seventh grader when the angel appeared to her.

That reality makes the angel's words "Do not be afraid" all the more understandable. Mary was engaged but not yet married, a virgin whose pregnancy would place her at enormous risk. She could lose her reputation, her marriage, her future, and possibly even her life. And it is this young girl, this overlooked, powerless person, who is told she will give birth to the very Son of God. It is hard to imagine the fear, confusion, and disbelief racing through her mind. An angelic visit alone would have been overwhelming. The message that followed was earth-shattering. Mary certainly was not expecting this. She had no reason to believe that anything extraordinary would ever happen to her.

So while we may enter the Christmas season with our own expectations about joy, peace, family, and tradition, Mary's story reminds us that the first Christmas was built entirely on the unexpected. Let's take a closer look at some of the unexpected things Mary encountered in this moment.

First, Mary did not expect a backward pregnancy announcement. In our culture, pregnancy announcements are often carefully planned and creatively shared. Social media has turned them into events, with photos, videos, clever captions, and themed reveals. Even my wife and I got caught up in making sure our own announcement was just right. Typically, the order is clear: The mother knows first, then the father, then close family, and finally the world.

But Mary's experience turns all of that upside down. She learns she is pregnant not through a test or a feeling but through an angel of God. She is told before her body has changed, before Joseph knows, before anyone else has a clue. And she is not just told that she is pregnant but that she will give birth to the Son of the Most High. Nothing about this happens in the "right" order.

What makes this even more surprising is who Mary is. She is not powerful or prominent. She is not spiritually elite. There is nothing outwardly remarkable about her. And yet God chooses her, not despite her ordinariness, but because of it. God is not drawn to her résumé but to her heart. Mary is humble, faithful, and open to God's leading. She does not try to dictate how she will serve God; she simply offers herself. Her lack of expectations about what faithfulness should look like makes her the perfect vessel for God's work. Her humility keeps pride at bay and leaves room for obedience.

This is consistent with God's pattern throughout Scripture. God consistently lifts up the lowly and blesses those the world overlooks. Jesus chooses his disciples not from the religious elite but from fishermen, laborers, and sinners. God has a heart for the lost, the outcast, and the humble. At the core of this is God's opposition to pride and love for humility.

This should challenge us. Many of us live lives of relative comfort. We have security, resources, opportunity, and stability. If the world has not humbled us, then Scripture invites us to humble ourselves before God. Because pride does real damage. Pride separates us from others and from God. It convinces us we deserve more, that we are better, that we can stand on our own. Pride shows up in impatience, entitlement, and harshness toward others. God humbles the proud—but it is far better for us to choose humility ourselves.

Like Mary, we find favor with God not through achievement but through surrender. When we put others first and center our lives on God, grace begins to shape us.

Finally, Mary did not expect to share that grace with the world. In bearing Jesus, Mary delivers more than a child; she delivers grace itself. Jesus is the embodiment of God's undeserved love, revealed through his life, death, and resurrection. Most of the gifts we exchange at Christmas are reciprocal. They come with expectations, obligations, or assumptions. Grace is different. Grace is given freely.

We fail constantly. We fall short again and again. And yet God forgives, restores, frees, and redeems. God's love does not run out or give up. That is the grace revealed in Jesus. And that grace is meant to transform us, turning fearful people into hopeful ones, prideful people into humble ones, and broken people into vessels of love.

Mary shares grace with the world by bringing Jesus into it. And we are called to do the same by living like him. Grace is the Christmas gift we are meant to give freely. When we offer mercy, kindness, love, or generosity to someone who does not deserve it or expect it, both giver and receiver are changed. That is where the heart of God is revealed.

Christmas should not just be a season of expectation and possibility. It should be a season of grace transactions. Imagine what this season would look like if we stopped keeping score. Imagine offering grace to the people who irritate us, frustrate us, or challenge us—the grinches, the difficult relatives, the people we label as enemies. The poor, the addict, the refugee, the stranger. What would it look like to give love without first deciding who deserves it?

So this Christmas, let us share grace freely, openly, and abundantly. Let us put down our expectations and pick up humility. Let us make this a Christmas that changes us, not just one that makes us feel nostalgic.

- What expectations do you have for this season? Are they realistic?
- How do you see God at work in the lives of those you don't expect God to work through? How does that affect your opinion of them and God?
- Challenge yourself to share grace this season. How can you offer three different people grace this week?

DAY 17

JOSEPH

An angel of the Lord appeared to Joseph in a dream and said, "Get up, take the child and his mother, and flee to Egypt, and remain there until I tell you, for Herod is about to search for the child, to destroy him." Then Joseph got up, took the child and his mother by night, and went to Egypt and remained there until the death of Herod. . . .

When Herod died, an angel of the Lord suddenly appeared in a dream to Joseph in Egypt and said, "Get up, take the child and his mother, and go to the land of Israel, for those who were seeking the child's life are dead." Then Joseph got up, took the child and his mother, and went to the land of Israel.

Matthew 2:13-15, 19-21

When I think about the sacrifices that Joseph makes for his wife, a child that bears his name but not his genes, and for the kingdom of God, I am consistently blown away. He reminds me of my hardworking grandparents on both sides of my family, who spent their lives in service to their children and community, working to make lives better for those around them, and wanting their children to do even better than they did. Here is a man who gets engaged to a young woman, expecting a wife who will join him in building a home and a family. A future filled with children, life, and love. There is no way that he could have thought that any of this would happen and that his faith would be stretched like it was.

Not only does Joseph have to accept the word of the angelic messenger that his life is about to be turned upside down but he also has to act quickly when his family is endangered. He learns through another angel of the threat to Jesus's life and leaps into action. This man's faith is ever present, ever steady, and ever true. He faithfully leads his family into a time of sojourn. We often think of sojourning, being displaced, uprooted, or exiled, as something entirely negative. We associate it with loss, instability, fear, and grief. And to be fair, those things are often very real companions on the journey. But when we turn to Scripture, we discover that God has a long history of working through the sojourns of ordinary people like you and me to bring life, love, peace, and even joy. Time and again, God meets people not when they are settled and secure but when they are on the move, uncertain of what lies ahead.

Joseph teaches us so beautifully how to live as disciples in times of sojourn: We need to face the darkness with obedience and faithfulness.

Three times, Joseph hears a word from God in a dream—once that Mary is pregnant, a second time to flee to Egypt, and a third time to return from there. Three times, Joseph responds with action. He does not argue. He does not demand explanations. He simply obeys. This does not mean Joseph is fearless; it means he is faithful. He trusts that God's guidance, even when it disrupts his plans, is leading him toward life.

So often, when we finally acknowledge the darkness in our lives, we try to manage it on our own. We distract ourselves. We numb ourselves. We escape however we can, through entertainment, spending, food, alcohol, or endless busyness. But none of these things actually deliver us. They may dull the pain for a moment, but they cannot heal it.

Joseph shows us a different way. He listens. He trusts. He obeys. Faithfulness does not always mean understanding what God is doing; it means taking the next right step when God speaks. Sometimes obedience looks like generosity when resources feel tight. Sometimes it looks like reaching out when staying silent would be easier. Sometimes it looks like changing course entirely because God is leading us somewhere new. Obedience does not remove the darkness—it opens us to the light of God's presence within it.

And finally, Joseph reminds us of the truth that makes everything else possible: God is with us in the sojourn.

God does not send Joseph, Mary, and Jesus into Egypt alone. God goes with them. God protects them. God delivers them. And God does the same for us. Whether we feel displaced right now or not, the truth is that we are all sojourners. This world is not our final home. We were created for life with God, and until that day, we live in between, moving, growing, longing, and hoping.

The good news of Advent is that God does not wait for us at the destination. God meets us on the road. God is with us when we are afraid. God is with us when we are grieving. God is with us when we are confused, tired, angry, or unsure. God is with us when we feel lost, and God is with us when we feel brave enough to keep going.

When we finally connect with the God who so desperately wants to be with us, something shifts. We begin to feel at home, even in unfamiliar places. We discover that joy and peace are not manufactured emotions but gifts rooted in God's nearness. The darkness does not disappear, but it no longer has the final word. Joseph teaches us that this is possible, as his faithful obedience leads him closer to God.

So, siblings in Christ, let us learn from Joseph. Let us not be afraid of the sojourn. Let us listen for God's voice, trust God's leading, and remember that we never walk alone.

- What part of Joseph's story stirs you the most? What obstacle that he faced would have been the hardest to overcome for you?
- Are you feeling like a sojourner in this season? How can God join you in that journey?
- How can you be more obedient to your calling today?

DAY 18

THE INNKEEPER

All went to their own towns to be registered. Joseph also went from the town of Nazareth in Galilee to Judea, to the city of David called Bethlehem, because he was descended from the house and family of David. He went to be registered with Mary, to whom he was engaged and who was expecting a child. While they were there, the time came for her to deliver her child. And she gave birth to her firstborn son and wrapped him in bands of cloth and laid him in a manger, because there was no place in the guest room.

Luke 2:3-7

My mother grew up as the youngest of five children, her oldest sibling being born twenty years before her. Tragically, this oldest child died in infancy in the middle of the Great Depression, and my mother never knew her. But she loved her older brother, twelve years her senior, and her oldest sister, almost seventeen years older. Then there was Aunt Carolyn, who for the ten years prior to my mother's arrival had been the "baby" of the family. The way I heard it was that Carolyn resented my mother for coming along and ruining her status as the youngest one and stealing attention from their parents. I don't know the validity of all of that, but I do know that from the moment I can remember there did seem to be some division between Carolyn, her husband, Dick, and the rest of the family.

Carolyn had lived a difficult life, including a hard divorce that left her as a single parent for a time. Unlike for her siblings, secondary education wasn't in the cards for her. She worked mostly blue-collar jobs, and Dick drove an eighteen-wheeler for a living. Their home was modest, and their lifestyle was just a little bit different from the rest of the family. Carolyn was rough around the edges and pulled no punches, and all of the softness of her family was given to her brothers and sisters. Let's just say that Aunt Carolyn wasn't my favorite aunt, and rather than looking forward to spending time with her, I often dreaded it.

That is why I will never forget my sick day with Aunt Carolyn. I was around nine or ten and had strep throat. I felt pretty awful and needed to stay home from school. It was the third day in a row that I needed to do so, and apparently my parents were out of PTO days because the day before I had gone to Aunt Pat's house to have her take care of me. Pat was my mom's oldest sister, and Pat and I loved each other like grandmother and grandson. My day with her was amazing, but apparently she couldn't keep me the next day, so Mom had to call Carolyn to see if I could stay with her. I remember standing by my mom as she called from the phone in the kitchen, hoping to hear that Carolyn was unavailable, but instead she agreed, and I was off to the mobile home park to spend the day with her. The whole way there, I was filled with uncertainty and fear. I was already counting down the hours until my mom could come get me again.

But friends, let me tell you, Carolyn was amazing. She had prepared my favorite foods and treats and shepherded me to a warm couch and several movies she had checked out from the library for me to watch. She catered to me all day with grace and love and helped me feel so much better. Our relationship changed that day, and I appreciated her in a whole new way. Sure, she wasn't as successful in her career as Uncle Don, or as loving as Aunt Pat, but she knew how to be there when it counted, and that mattered deeply.

I think of Carolyn when I think of the innkeeper. So often, we present the innkeeper as some greedy and evil person who forced a pregnant woman into a cave. I can remember in almost every children's Christmas pageant or Sunday school animated film that the innkeeper was portrayed as a mean and angry man. He refused to be kind to a couple on the brink, a negative image quite like the one I had of Aunt Carolyn.

But in reality, it wasn't an innkeeper at all. The word Luke uses that is most famously translated as "room for them in the inn" is *katalyma*, which speaks more to a guest room in a family home than it does a spot at a professional hotel. In fact, it's the same word Luke uses in describing the upper room, where Jesus and the disciples gathered for the Last Supper. In the case of Mary and Joseph, this guest room was in a home and was filled by other family members—perhaps members of Joseph's family since this was his ancestral town—traveling for the Roman census. This was the reason that Mary and Joseph had to head into what was the ancient equivalent of the garage to give birth to Jesus.

But just like Aunt Carolyn, it turns out the "innkeeper" tried their best to be as welcoming and accommodating as possible, providing the best they could for a family member in need. In a moment when their home and hospitality were needed, they did everything they could. Their home was already filled to the brim; when they saw others in need, they made accommodations and welcomed in the Christ Child.

Maybe there is a person in your life like the innkeeper, whose first impression was one of negativity, fear, and anger, to whom you need to offer a second chance. A chance to show you their heart filled with love and grace. Maybe you didn't make the best first impression with someone and you need to go out of your way to mend that relationship and show your true love for others. This season is one in which we can each offer the gift of grace to one another, opening doors with faithful hospitality. Who knows, in welcoming others into our hearts and lives, we may be making room for Christ to take up residence in our hearts and lives.

- Have you had a family member like Aunt Carolyn, whose kindness turned your heart to a new understanding?
- How can you be more welcoming of those whom you might have written off as rude or mean? What steps can you take to invite them into your heart and life?
- How can you go above and beyond to love others this season?

DAY 19

THE SHEPHERDS

The angel said to them, "Do not be afraid, for see, I am bringing you good news of great joy for all the people: to you is born this day in the city of David a Savior, who is the Messiah, the Lord. This will be a sign for you: you will find a child wrapped in bands of cloth and lying in a manger." And suddenly there was with the angel a multitude of the heavenly host, praising God and saying,

"Glory to God in the highest heaven,
and on earth peace among those whom he favors!"

When the angels had left them and gone into heaven, the shepherds said to one another, "Let us go now to Bethlehem and see this thing that has taken place, which the Lord has made known to us."

Luke 2:10-15

Once, for a brief and humbling season of my life, I was a shepherd. Or more accurately, a temporary goatherd.

In high school, I worked at Uncle Jack's Feed and Farm Supply at what was at the time the very western edge of my hometown, Little Rock. Uncle Jack's now unfortunately no longer exists, as the city continued to grow out to what was formerly farmland, taking away the need for a farm supply store. But at the time, my job was mostly what you'd expect: loading and unloading heavy sacks of horse and cattle feed, sweeping floors, and doing whatever odd jobs needed to be done. One of those odd jobs, however, was especially odd.

Uncle Jack owned several uncleared acres of land around the store, and he decided it needed to be cleaned up. He could have rented a tractor or hired someone with a bush hog, but instead he chose what he believed to be the most efficient method: goats. Goats, as it turns out, will eat just about anything. That meant my task was to build fences, place the goats inside them, wait until the brush was cleared, and then move the goats to a new location. This process went on for months.

Everything about that job was manageable, except moving the goats. Goats do not like being relocated. You can't reason with them; you can't pull them. And the billy goat? He was the worst of them all. Eventually, the only way to get the job done was to pick them up one by one and carry them while I was being kicked, squirmed on, and occasionally bitten. It was exhausting, frustrating, and far less romantic than any image you might have of shepherding.

Every time I read about the shepherds in Luke's Gospel, I think about those goats. And I can't help but assuming the shepherds we encounter in the Christmas story had a job that was probably tougher and more dangerous than what I had to do in high school.

To understand their story, we turn to Luke 2:8-20, where shepherds are keeping watch over their flocks by night when heaven suddenly breaks into their ordinary, difficult work. An angel appears. The glory of the Lord shines around them, and they, like Zechariah and Joseph and Mary before them, are terrified. And then come the words that change everything: "Do not be afraid, for see, I am bringing you good news of great joy for all the people" (2:10).

When I think of the shepherds, I also think of Carolyn's husband, Dick, the truck driver. The man behind the inglorious job, living on the road, away from family and friends so often. It's a job that all the rest of us so deeply depend upon when we go to the grocery store or head to Walmart. Without the truck drivers, those shelves don't stay quite as full, but we often fail to appreciate the men and women behind the wheel. Likewise, shepherds had an important social function. They had a tough but vital job for their economy and way of life, often traveling far out in the fields, away from their homes and families. It might have been easy to forget the shepherds were out there, and still are today in some places, quietly going about their business and tending to their flocks.

But when the news of the Messiah arrives, the heavens do not open above the palace. The announcement does not go first to priests, kings, or scholars. Instead, God shows up in a field and tells the people there they are part of the story. They are told what has happened and what they would find in town and are left to respond however they see fit.

And they certainly do respond. They respond with haste: "Let us go now to Bethlehem" (2:15). I imagine them checking house after house, peering into dark corners, asking awkward questions, until they finally find a baby lying in a feeding trough, just as they were told. This is what grace looks like. God does not wait for people to clean themselves up before extending an invitation. God comes first and then invites us to come and see. And in fact, Jesus makes that very invitation to come and see frequently in his ministry.

Whether or not you expect God to do anything in your life this season, you are invited. Whether you feel spiritually confident or painfully uncertain, you are invited. Whether you see yourself as faithful or flawed, deserving or disqualified, God invites you to come and meet him. And like the shepherds, we are also invited to extend that invitation to others—to friends, family members, neighbors, strangers. Love comes down at Christmas, and it does not come quietly or selectively. It comes for everyone.

When the shepherds return to their fields, nothing about their circumstances has changed. They still have sheep to guard. They still have the same heat, cold, rain, and sun to face every day. And yet everything is different. They return glorifying and praising God because they now carry a new identity. The world may still see them as shepherds, but they know who they are. They are witnesses. They are bearers of good news. They are people who have seen God with their own eyes. Their expectations have been reshaped, and that shift changes how they see themselves and their lives.

The same is true for us. When we begin to expect God to move, when we believe that God might actually work in and through our ordinary, imperfect lives, it changes us. We stop defining ourselves by our failures, our labels, or our past. We begin to see ourselves as God sees us: beloved children, worthy of God's presence not because of what we have done but because of who God is.

As we walk this Advent journey, let us remember the shepherds. The first to hear the good news. The first to run toward the light. The first to realize that God's love is not reserved for the powerful or the polished.

- When have you felt like the shepherds, perhaps unseen or underappreciated? What did God do for you in that moment?
- Whom do you think the shepherds are in our society today? How might we help them feel more loved and included?
- How can we respond to God's invitations in the same excitement the shepherds modeled?

DAY 20

THE MAGI

Magi from the east came to Jerusalem, asking, "Where is the child who has been born king of the Jews? For we observed his star in the east and have come to pay him homage." When King Herod heard this, he was frightened, and all Jerusalem with him. . . .

When they saw that the star had stopped, they were overwhelmed with joy. On entering the house, they saw the child with Mary his mother, and they knelt down and paid him homage. Then, opening their treasure chests, they offered him gifts of gold, frankincense, and myrrh. And having been warned in a dream not to return to Herod, they left for their own country by another road.

Matthew 2:1-3, 10-12

There were several times in my childhood when I found myself standing on a church stage or a school cafeteria riser wrapped in my dad's robe or an extra sheet from the linen closet, participating in a nativity play. Every little girl hoped to be Mary, holding the baby Jesus, or the angel dressed in white and gold, delivering the good news. Most of my guy friends wanted to be shepherds. They got to carry staffs, wave them around, and maybe even smack one another with them. But me? I always wanted to be one of the wise men. They had the best costumes, the brightest colors, the coolest hats, the boxes wrapped in shiny paper. They were mysterious and important; they were the showmen. And if I'm being honest, that's exactly who I wanted to be.

That memory has stayed with me. Every year on Epiphany, when the church tells the story of the magi arriving to see the Christ Child, I can still picture myself as that kid in bright blue fabric, clutching a gold box, kneeling before Jesus. Even now, something about their story captures my imagination.

They arrive from the east, guided by a star, asking a dangerous question: "Where is the child who has been born king of the Jews?" (2:2). Their question unsettles King Herod, disrupts Jerusalem, and ultimately leads them to a small house where they encounter not just a child but the king of the world.

Over the centuries, we've added layers to how we imagine these figures. In popular culture and Christmas card theology, they are almost always three kings, riding camels beneath a starry sky. That image was cemented in the church's imagination in 1857, when John Henry Hopkins Jr. wrote the Christmas carol "We Three Kings," originally for a nativity play. But throughout the centuries, tradition filled in the gaps Scripture left open. By around the sixth century, the magi were given names—Caspar, Melchior, and Balthazar—and were imagined as kings from different kingdoms, symbolizing the whole world coming to Christ.

Visual artists took these ideas and extended them in depictions of the Adoration of the Magi, the moment when the wise men lay out gifts before Jesus. These scenes allowed them to showcase all of their skills: painting human faces, exotic clothing, animals, architecture, and landscapes.

One of my favorite depictions comes from Albrecht Dürer, a deeply faithful German artist. His painting is filled with theological symbolism: Mary robed in blue, the most expensive pigment, emphasizing her significance; Jesus reaching outward toward the magi, already offering love; a self-portrait of Dürer himself among the worshipers, reminding us that every generation is invited into the story. There are symbols everywhere in the painting, including pillars of cloud echoing the Exodus, insects and plants pointing toward death and resurrection, stones and butterflies foreshadowing Easter. The message is clear: Even here, at the manger, the whole gospel is already present.

But art and tradition aside, who were the magi really, and why do they matter?

The word *magi* is Persian in origin. These were not kings but royal officials, advisors, scholars, astrologers—men who studied the heavens to discern the movements of the present that might be shaping history. They likely served in the court of the Persian king, interpreting signs and advising rulers. When they saw a new star rise in the west, they understood it as the birth announcement of a king. And so, they were sent not just as curious observers but as envoys, carrying gifts worthy of royalty. Their journey was long, expensive, and dangerous. This was not a sweet stroll to the manger. It was a diplomatic mission we can imagine as involving a large caravan, possibly dozens of people, crossing borders and walking straight into political tension, with Herod now fearful about what their arrival and report of a star rising to mark the birth of a king means.

Yet the magi continue. Led again by the star, they arrive not at a palace but at a home. And when they see the child, something shifts, and they worship him. These outsiders, foreigners, astrologers—men beyond Israel's covenant—recognize what many insiders miss. Jesus is not just King of the Jews. He is Lord of all. And in that moment, the gospel cracks open wide enough for the whole world to step inside.

And it is what happens next that is most important: The magi teach us what it truly means to adore Christ. First, they show us that worship begins with joy. Matthew tells us that when they saw the star stop, "they were overwhelmed with joy" (2:10). This is not polite happiness or restrained reverence. It is overwhelming joy, the kind that spills out when hope is fulfilled. Worship does not require us to deny our burdens, but it does invite us to lay them down. When we worship Jesus, we are reminded that guilt does not get the final word, fear does not reign forever, and stress is not the center of the universe. Joy rises when we remember who God is and what God has done.

Second, the magi model humility. These powerful men kneel, they bow, and they acknowledge that their authority, knowledge, and status mean nothing in the presence of Christ. True worship always humbles us. It reminds us that the world does not revolve around us and that surrender is not weakness but wisdom.

Finally, they offer gifts. Gold for a king. Frankincense for worship. Myrrh, a burial spice, pointing toward the cross. Their gifts are costly and symbolic, but more than that, they are personal. They give what they have. We may not bring gold or incense, but we are still called to offer Christ our gifts, our time, our energy, our resources, our obedience. Worship is not only sung; it is lived. It shows up in generosity, in service, in hospitality, in faithfulness.

O come let us adore him—like the magi did.

- How have you viewed the magi in the past? How do you see them now?
- As we near the end of Advent, how does the guidance they model shape how you will worship this season?
- What gifts can you offer Christ in the remainder of Advent?

DAY 21

HERODE

When Herod saw that he had been tricked by the magi, he was infuriated, and he sent and killed all the children in and around Bethlehem who were two years old or under, according to the time that he had learned from the magi. Then what had been spoken through the prophet Jeremiah was fulfilled:

"A voice was heard in Ramah,
wailing and loud lamentation,
Rachel weeping for her children;
she refused to be consoled, because they are no more."

Matthew 2:16-18

Herod the Great is one of the most fascinating, and terrifying, figures surrounding the story of Jesus's birth. His name echoes through the Christmas narrative like a dark undertone beneath the angel songs and starlit skies. While we often rush past him on our way to the manger, Herod deserves our attention because his response to Jesus exposes something deeply human, and deeply dangerous. He might not be someone we would invite over for Christmas dinner, but he is a part of this story, and we must take him seriously.

Much of what we know about Herod comes from the Roman-Jewish historian Josephus, who describes a man not born into royalty but one who seized power through ambition, political maneuvering, and ruthless violence. Herod was the younger son of a similarly ambitious government official, and through determination and force of will, he climbed the ranks of Roman politics. As Rome tightened its grip on Israel, Herod aligned himself closely with the empire, becoming a trusted client king.

When Rome backed Herod's campaign against King Antigonus, the last Hasmonean (Maccabean) king of Judea, the result was a brutal three-year war. When it finally ended, Herod emerged victorious and crowned himself king in Jerusalem. A social climber and canny political leader, Herod ruled for thirty-seven years.

But his reign was anything but peaceful. He governed through fear, swiftly and violently crushing any hint of rebellion. He was known for extravagant building projects, including a massive renovation of the temple, but also for paranoia, cruelty, and bloodshed. Herod fought hard to gain power, and he fought even harder to keep it. As mentioned yesterday, this was the reason for his negative response to the arrival of the wise men.

Herod's fear was quiet, cold, and dangerous. His fear came from what he believed this newborn king would mean for him. Herod heard the word *king* and immediately saw everything in terms of loss. Loss of power and control. Loss of his carefully constructed kingdom. His expectations of Jesus were shaped entirely by fear, and that fear drove him to horrific sin. Matthew records the massacre of the infants (2:16), one of the most evil acts in Scripture, committed by a man desperate to protect his throne. Fear of loss is a powerful force, and if we're honest, that same fear lives in us too.

There are moments—quiet ones we don't always admit—when we resist the idea of Jesus truly being King of our lives. Because if Jesus is King, then we are not, and that means something has to give. We might lose our own sense of control, or we might lose our comfort or our carefully guarded security. We might have to let go of guilt we've grown used to carrying or shame that has shaped our identity. We might have to release our judgment, our grudges, our need to be right. If I'm really honest, there are times I want to do things my way, not Christ's way. I want to wear the crown, and so did Herod.

Herod expected Jesus to be a threat, but he never expected Jesus to be good news. And yet, that is exactly what the angels proclaimed. To the shepherds they said, "I am bringing you good news of great joy for all the people" (Luke 2:10). *All the people.* Not just the faithful, not just the humble—all people.

Even violent, broken rulers like Herod—actually, especially people like Herod. And people like us. Jesus came to save Herod just as much as he came to save you and me. That truth sits at the very heart of what John Wesley, the founder of Methodism, called prevenient grace. In the most simple terms, this means that before we know anything about God or our need for God's love, God is already moving toward us. God is already seeking relationship and reaching out, offering salvation, even when we run from it, ignore it, or fear what it will cost us.

Herod couldn't see that Jesus's arrival was good news for him. His fear blinded him. And fear still does that today. There are seasons when Christ's coming doesn't feel like good news, when it feels inconvenient, disruptive, or demanding. But, friends, we are mistaken in those moments, forgetting the depth of what Christ can do and has done for us. The coming of Jesus is always good news. His birth in a manger two thousand years ago was good news. His coming into our hearts now, to heal us, forgive us, and remake us, is still good news.

Yes, accepting Jesus as King means that some things will be lost. Some habits must change. Some identities must die. Some crowns must be laid down. But what we receive in return is infinitely better than anything we could build for ourselves. A life centered on Christ is richer in meaning, deeper in love, and steadier in hope than a life spent clinging to control. Why would we settle for the brokenness of this world when Christ offers abundance? Why would we exhaust ourselves trying to hold power like water slipping through our fingers when Jesus offers freedom instead? Why would we fight for dominance when God calls us into joyful service—loving others with the matchless love of Christ?

Herod chose fear. The magi chose worship. The shepherds chose obedience. The question Advent places before us is simple but piercing: How will we respond to the coming of Jesus not just at Christmas but all year long? This season invites us to trade our old ways for the new life Christ brings. To lay down fear and take up faith. To loosen our grip on comfort and live fully into our calling. To stop running from grace and allow ourselves to be found by God. Sisters and brothers, may we not be led by fear but guided by faith. Jesus Christ is coming. May we open our hearts and greet our King.

- When or where in your life are you most like Herod, clinging for power and control?
- When do you cling for control the most? What motivates this?
- How can we respond to Christ's coming by surrendering our hearts to him?

DAY 22

SIMEON

Now there was a man in Jerusalem whose name was Simeon; this man was righteous and devout, looking forward to the consolation of Israel, and the Holy Spirit rested on him. It had been revealed to him by the Holy Spirit that he would not see death before he had seen the Lord's Messiah. Guided by the Spirit, Simeon came into the temple, and when the parents brought in the child Jesus to do for him what was customary under the law, Simeon took him in his arms and praised God, saying,

> *"Master, now you are dismissing your servant in peace,*
> *according to your word,*
> *for my eyes have seen your salvation,*
> *which you have prepared in the presence of all peoples,*
> *a light for revelation to the gentiles*
> *and for glory to your people Israel."*

Luke 2:25-32

Earlier, I mentioned a cool, older cousin of mine. You may remember that he was handsome, smart, hardworking, and successful. He was also kind enough to tolerate a much younger and much less cool me. It is no accident that he is the way he is, though, because his father is special as well. His dad is my dad's first cousin, although they grew up more like brothers. My grandmother died when my dad was a young man, and his aunt took up the mantle of raising him. So, this cousin of my father has always felt more like an uncle. He is a good, kind, and gentle man, one I admire and respect.

He has long served his community as a criminal defense attorney, a difficult job to be sure. He has represented people who have committed heinous crimes, people we can't imagine being in the same room with, much less having a relationship with. He sees this role as a mission, his service, to defend the innocent, but also to maintain the checks and balances of justice to make sure that everyone gets their fair shot. He has an ability to clearly see the truth of the work in front of him, and he serves with compassion and fairness.

But it is his vision that I admire most. My uncle has the ability to see past the surface and look to the deeper truths of any given situation. He can see past the muck and the mire into the beauty. More than just seeing it, he is quick to name it and celebrate the truth when it is discovered, both at work and in his personal life. We are drawn to him because he so powerfully articulates the good news of God's majesty, found in sunsets, great meals, and close connections with others. It is the gift of sight that he shines brightly.

That is the gift of Simeon. This righteous and devout man, filled with the Holy Spirit, who has been promised by God that he won't die until he meets the Messiah. I love the image of him encountering Mary and Joseph with the only days-old Jesus. Imagine: a bearded, aged stranger approaching a young family, taking their child into his arms, and then publicly praising God. I can see Mary trying to kindly hold Jesus back, but Simeon is insisting, making the case that he can see what God was doing.

And boy could he see. His gift, like my uncle's, was the ability to see. Simeon had been told he would live to see the Messiah, the triumphant King of God. I am sure that he was expecting and looking for what most other Jews were at the time, a mighty warrior or a political upheaval. His eyes were peeled for action, excitement, violence. But thanks to the Holy Spirit, he has the ability to see that God isn't bringing salvation in the form of strength but in quite the opposite way, in the vulnerable gift of a baby.

It is this gift of clear vision that we need to unlock today. For we are in the final stretch of the Christmas season. The pressure is really pouring on. We are checking our lists, making the last-minute shopping trips, organizing our menus, and getting all packed to travel. We may be feeling the pressure that the month has slipped by us, and we haven't had that magical Christmas moment yet. We may be experiencing loneliness, fear, dread, or flat-out exhaustion. But the truth is, if we can tap into the powers of vision held by my uncle and Simeon, we can begin to see the beauty and majesty of God in all of it. While it may not be what we want or what we are expecting, God is in it. For this is the season of Immanuel, God with us.

I think that the reason my uncle and Simeon see the world so clearly is because they look intently. My uncle works hard to see the truth, turning over stones and waiting for the waters to clear. Simeon was always on the lookout, hoping to see a sign of God's coming salvation. The good news for you and me is that this is not some gift we are born with or without but a skill we can hone through intentional practice. We can look a little longer, think a little deeper, and see where God is moving, even if it isn't clear at first.

- When have you struggled to see the beauty of a situation through the muck and mire of life?

- When have you been able to clearly see what God is doing in and through you, despite any distractions?
- How can you work to clarify your sight today to embrace the beauty of God with us in this season?

DAY 23

ANNA

There was also a prophet, Anna the daughter of Phanuel, of the tribe of Asher. She was of a great age, having lived with her husband seven years after her marriage, then as a widow to the age of eighty-four. She never left the temple but worshiped there with fasting and prayer night and day. At that moment she came and began to praise God and to speak about the child to all who were looking for the redemption of Jerusalem.

Luke 2:36-38

My wife has a remarkable gift for bringing joy and sharing it with others. She has a way of making a turkey and cheese sandwich feel like a Michelin-star meal without ever making it feel stiff. Everything she does is thoughtful, meant to bring happiness and love to those around her. She is light and love personified, and she shines her light on all. She is graceful and kind, classy and composed. Maybe you have encountered someone like this. When you walk through their door, you are not simply there; you are seen and you are welcomed. You are reminded that your presence matters.

But what makes her personality so powerful is not simply what she does for others directly. It is that she genuinely delights in celebrating the goodness of God. She gives thanks easily and publicly and she draws attention to blessings that others might overlook. She has trained her heart to notice grace, and because she notices it, she celebrates it. And because she celebrates it, everyone else in the room begins to see it too. Whenever I read about Anna in Luke 2, I think of her.

Anna appears in the temple just after Mary and Joseph bring the infant Jesus to present him to the Lord. Luke tells us that she was a prophet, the daughter of Phanuel, of the tribe of Asher. One of only a handful of female prophets in the Bible, Anna plays a key role here. She had been married only seven years before becoming a widow, and she is now very old, having lived decades without her husband. The fact that she never left the temple but worshiped there with fasting and prayer night and day speaks not only to her piety but also that she probably didn't have any children to care for her. She may have been truly alone. In just a few verses, Luke sketches the portrait of a woman whose entire life had become an offering of devotion in spite of her brokenness.

It would have been easy for Anna's story to turn bitter. She had known loss. She had known long years of waiting in a world still aching under Roman occupation, still longing for the redemption of Israel. She had prayed prayers that stretched on for decades. She had watched generation after generation come and go while she remained in the temple courts, worshiping, fasting, and hoping. And yet what stands out about Anna is not sorrow but orientation. Her life was oriented toward the goodness of God. She had dedicated herself not merely to religious activity but to attentiveness. Through years of worship and prayer, she had cultivated the kind of heart that anticipates God's faithfulness.

So when Mary and Joseph walked into the temple carrying a baby who looked like every other baby, Anna recognized what others did not. In this short story about her, she models something truly powerful for us to live into today. In three simple movements, Anna shows us what it looks like to share our faith in a way that is both natural and powerful.

First, she recognized the goodness of God. Recognition is not accidental; it is practiced and formed over time. Anna, like Simeon, was able to see what was happening in that moment because she had spent years training her eyes to look for the work of God. The long discipline of prayer had sharpened her spiritual vision. She had not allowed waiting to dull her expectation. Instead, waiting had deepened it; so when the promise finally stood before her in the baby Jesus, she did not miss it. There is something deeply instructive here. Anna reminds us that if we dedicate ourselves to the goodness of God, if we shape our lives around worship, gratitude, and hope, we begin to see grace more clearly. We begin to recognize Christ in places we might otherwise overlook. As the old saying goes, "We see what we are looking for." If you start thinking about red cars, you will see red cars. The same rings true for the things of God.

Second, Anna celebrated publicly and gave thanks. Luke tells us that she began praising God. There is no indication that she pulled Mary aside for a quiet theological conversation. She did not keep her joy contained. She responded openly, verbally, and with gratitude. After decades of prayer for redemption, she stood in the temple and thanked God out loud for what she had seen. That kind of celebration changes a room. It shifts the atmosphere. It draws others into awareness.

In the same way my wife's gratitude at a dinner table lifts everyone's hearts toward thankfulness, Anna's praise would have turned heads in the temple courts. And when someone genuinely delights in the goodness of God, it gives others permission to do the same. Faith that is only private is incomplete. Gratitude that is never spoken cannot multiply.

Anna understood that when God's goodness is recognized, it deserves celebration.

Third, in keeping with this, Anna told others. She spoke about the child "to all who were looking for the redemption of Jerusalem" (2:38). I love that phrase, because it suggests that there were others who were waiting too. Others who were praying. Others who were wondering if God had forgotten his promises. Anna found them and said, in essence, *He's here.*

This is the full circle of faithful witness. We recognize the goodness of God. We celebrate it with thanksgiving. And then we share what we have seen and experienced with those who are still looking. Notice that Anna did not argue, coerce, or attempt to manufacture belief. She simply bore witness. She told others what she had encountered. That is still our calling today. We are not asked to force faith into anyone's life. We are asked to recognize Christ, give thanks for him, and speak honestly about what he has done.

When I think about my wife's personality and love, I realize that what she is really doing is creating space for people to taste and see the goodness of God. Her spirit, her intentionality, her gratitude—all of it points beyond herself. It invites others into celebration. It reminds us that life is a gift and that God is generous. Anna did the same thing in the temple that day.

After years of devotion, she recognized the gift standing in front of her. She celebrated it with praise, and she told others who were waiting.

In this season, and in every season of our lives, we are invited to follow her example. We can train our hearts to notice grace. We can choose to speak gratitude aloud. And we can gently, confidently tell others what we have seen. May we be people who dedicate ourselves to the goodness of God so fully that we do not miss him when he comes near. May our lives become tables set for celebration. And when we recognize Christ in our midst, may we praise boldly and share freely, trusting that there are others who are still looking for redemption and are longing to hear that he is here.

Over the next few days, you will probably have ample opportunities to do just these things. Imagine how dramatically you could affect the life of your family and friends if at your Christmas gatherings and celebrations you saw the goodness of God in them, praised God for it, and told them about it. Lives could be changed forever. Let's not wait any longer.

- Who in your family makes you feel the most loved and seen? What do they do that makes you feel like that?

- How can you be better at recognizing, praising, and telling about the goodness of God in your life? Does this come easily for you, or do you struggle?
- Name one person you will encounter in the next week that you can share the good news of God's activity with.

DAY 24

PAUL

Now as [Saul] was going along and approaching Damascus, suddenly a light from heaven flashed around him. He fell to the ground and heard a voice saying to him, "Saul, Saul, why do you persecute me?" He asked, "Who are you, Lord?" The reply came, "I am Jesus, whom you are persecuting. But get up and enter the city, and you will be told what you are to do." The men who were traveling with him stood speechless because they heard the voice but saw no one. Saul got up from the ground, and though his eyes were open, he could see nothing; so they led him by the hand and brought him into Damascus.

Acts 9:3-8

There are few types of storylines that capture the human heart quite like a redemption story. Whether it is a fictional character like Jean Valjean in *Les Misérables*, who rises from bitterness and imprisonment into mercy and sacrificial love, or a real figure like Nelson Mandela, who endured suffering and emerged committed to reconciliation rather than revenge, we are drawn to stories in which brokenness does not have the final word. We long to believe that people can change, that hatred can soften, that mistakes do not define everything for all time. Redemption stirs something deep within us because it whispers that perhaps our own failures are not final either.

And yet, as compelling as those stories are, none of them compares to the redemption story that began in a manger and explodes onto a dusty road outside Damascus. On Christmas Eve, we gather around a baby in a manger. We sing softly lit carols as we picture shepherds kneeling and angels shining. But we must not forget that the child we celebrate tonight grew into the risen Christ who confronts hatred, interrupts violence, and transforms enemies into ambassadors of grace. Christmas is not sentimental; it is redemptive. The baby in Bethlehem comes for moments like Paul's.

When we first meet Saul, who would later be known as Paul, in the Book of Acts, he is not a sympathetic figure. He is not misunderstood, and he is not simply confused. Scripture tells us plainly that he was breathing threats and murder against the disciples of the Lord. He actively sought permission to track down followers of Jesus, to bind them, drag them from their homes, and bring them to Jerusalem for punishment. He stood approvingly at the execution of

Stephen, the church's first martyr. Saul was not a passive bystander; he was an aggressive persecutor. It is important that we do not sanitize this part of his story. Saul was consumed by anger and convinced of his own righteousness. He believed he was defending truth. He believed he was protecting God. He was certain that this movement called "the Way" threatened everything he valued—his religious system, his worldview, the social structures that granted him power and influence. And like so many throughout history, he responded to perceived threat with force.

If we were reading his story for the first time, we would assume we know where it is headed. Saul is the villain, the cautionary tale. Saul is the one God will eventually judge. But God had something else in mind. As Saul traveled toward Damascus, intent on continuing his campaign of persecution, a light from heaven flashed around him, brighter than the midday sun. He fell to the ground and heard a voice call his name, "Saul, Saul," a double naming that echoes God's calls to Abraham, Jacob, and Moses, moments when history bends and a divine mission is given. And when Saul asks who is speaking, the answer is staggering: "I am Jesus, whom you are persecuting" (9:5).

It is the risen Christ who meets him. The same Jesus who once lay wrapped in swaddling cloths now stands in resurrected glory, confronting the man who has tried to erase his followers from the earth. And what is most remarkable is not simply that Jesus appears but that he is not there to condemn Saul, to punish him, or to destroy him. No, Jesus has come to redeem him.

Christmas Eve tells us why. The child born in Bethlehem is Immanuel, God with us, not only in our innocence but in our rebellion. Christ enters our lives not only when we are ready to receive him in our worship but when our hearts are bent toward violence. Christ comes into the world not because we are ready for him but because we desperately need him. He comes precisely for people like Saul.

Saul's encounter with Christ is confusing and disorienting. He rises from the ground unable to see. For three days, he neither eats nor drinks. The man who strode toward Damascus full of confidence must now be led by the hand. Everything he thought he understood has been shattered. And that is often how redemption begins, not with clarity, but with disruption. Not with certainty but with the painful realization that we were wrong. Many of us have had moments, though perhaps less dramatic, when God's presence interrupts our status quo. Perhaps it was a narrowly avoided accident or a conversation we did not expect. It may have been a conviction that settles heavily on our hearts. We can dismiss these as coincidence, or we can pause long enough to ask whether Christ is speaking.

On that Christmas night long ago, the world did not recognize what had happened. There was no headline in Rome. No announcement in Herod's palace. Just a baby, a manger, and a handful of witnesses. And yet that quiet birth set in motion a redemption that would one day stop a violent Pharisee in his tracks and turn him into the greatest missionary the church has ever known. Because this story is not merely about Saul being forgiven. It is about Saul being called.

Right after Paul's conversion, Jesus speaks to Ananias, a disciple in Damascus. He asks Ananias to go find Paul and help him regain his sight, but Ananias protests based on Paul's reputation as a persecutor of Christians.

Then Jesus says something astonishing: "He is an instrument whom I have chosen to bring my name before gentiles and kings and before the people of Israel" (Acts 9:15). The man who sought to silence the church would become its boldest preacher. The one who dragged believers from their homes would plant congregations across the Roman world. The persecutor would become the proclaimer. This is what Christmas makes possible. The manger leads to the cross. The cross leads to the resurrection. And the resurrection leads to redemption and commissioning. The child we worship tonight does not merely forgive sin; he transforms sinners into vessels of his grace.

If God can take a man like Saul, full of hatred, convinced of his own righteousness, complicit in violence, and reshape his life into something beautiful and world-changing, then none of us are beyond the reach of Christ. No past is too stained, no failure too final, no heart too hardened. Christmas Eve is not simply about remembering a birth; it is about trusting what that birth means. It means that light shines in the darkness, and the darkness cannot overcome it. It means that Christ steps into our world and into our stories not to condemn but to redeem and to call. So tonight, as we gather around candlelight and sing of silent nights and holy infants, let us remember that the baby in the manger comes for the road to Damascus. He comes for moments of interruption and awakening. He comes for enemies and skeptics and strivers. He comes for you and for me.

May we be willing to be interrupted. May we allow Christ to confront what needs confronting and heal what needs healing. And may we, like Paul, discover that redemption is not the end of the story but the beginning of a calling to become vessels who carry his light into a world still in need of Christmas.

- What other redemption stories can you think of? Which ones resonate with you?
- What has God called you to do in the world?
- What have you been redeemed from? What can you thank God for helping you leave behind?

DAY 25

JESUS

And the Word became flesh and lived among us, and we have seen his glory, the glory as of a father's only son, full of grace and truth.

John 1:14

After weeks of anticipation, Scripture, candles, songs, shepherds, angels, and long journeys, we arrive at the heart of it all. Christmas Day. Merry Christmas to you and to your family.

Today we have a chance to fully embrace and celebrate the gift of Christ, the Lord who enters our story to redeem and to save, to give the greatest gifts we could ever receive. I don't know how your day will be spent. I know that this year, I will have gotten home late from the 11 p.m. Christmas Eve service, and I will have put on *National Lampoon's Christmas Vacation* to watch one last time before falling asleep. I know that my kids will wake me up too early, and my loving wife will pour me a hot cup of coffee as we settle in to open presents and rejoice in the day. There will be chaos, shouting, paper flying, and love.

Maybe your morning will be a rushed exit to get to a family member's house or a quiet morning waiting for the grandkids to arrive.

However it looks, here is my Christmas prayer for you. I pray that as we have walked through the season of Advent together, gathering the stories of all the family members and important characters around the birth of Jesus, that you are fully ready to receive the gift that is the salvation of our Lord. I pray that we might learn to walk in the footsteps of our faith ancestors and our family ancestors, seeking faithfulness, obedience, and truth. I pray that this season would be one that changes us forever, leading us deeper into the love of God and more ready to connect with others. I pray that this has helped us love all of our families, however they come to us, more than we did before. I pray that we may all continue to build the family of God in the light of Christ with us.

So, my friends, Merry Christmas! May the love of God be always shed abroad in your hearts.